The Master Musicians Series

D0233919

MAHLER

Series edited by Stanley Sadie

THE MASTER MUSICIANS SERIES

MAHLER

by Michael Kennedy

*With eight pages of plates and
music examples in text*

J. M. DENT & SONS LTD
London & Melbourne

Made in Great Britain
by Garden City Press Ltd,
Letchworth, Herts
for
J. M. DENT & SONS LTD
Aldine House, 33 Welbeck Street, London W1M 8LX

Paperback edition 1977
Last reprinted 1985

British Library Cataloguing in Publication Data

Kennedy, Michael, 1926–
    Mahler. – (The Master musicians series)
    1. Mahler, Gustave   2. Composers – Austria
    I. Title   II. Series
    780'.92'4   ML410.M23

ISBN 0-460-02161-3

Preface

'We cannot see how any of his music can long survive him,' a New York critic wrote in 1911, a few days after Mahler's death. This short-sighted Olympian pronouncement will raise nothing but a derisive laugh today, when his music is popular to a degree that no one could have foreseen even twenty years ago. But Mahlerians must not exaggerate the extent of his neglect in the years from 1911 to about 1960. A devoted group of conductors, several of whom had known Mahler—among them Klemperer, Mengelberg, Walter, Bodanzky and Fried—kept his name before the public. Research shows that there were more performances than is perhaps realized. These devotees kept the pot simmering, as it were, so that when the time came for the gas to be fully turned up, the contents came quickly to the boil. Less fortunate composers have had to start from stone-cold.

The critical rehabilitation of Mahler's reputation is a fascinating study. There have always been impassioned champions of his cause, but for nearly half a century they were a minority. The musical atmosphere in England during my adolescence was predominantly anti-Mahler. He was not to be taken seriously. Mr Donald Mitchell has written of how a leading critic of yesteryear said to him: 'We don't want Mahler here,' and I could give a parallel example from my own experience. It is a warning to critics to temper their judgments with humility; no doubt many of those to whom Mahler is now an open book are guilty of misjudging some other composer as he was misjudged. What was particularly heinous in his case was that many adverse verdicts were recorded on the sparsest of acquaintance with the music. There was also an attitude among the arbiters of English taste which implied the most extraordinary choices: if you liked Stravinsky, you couldn't like Mahler; if you liked Mahler, you couldn't like Vaughan Williams; even, if you liked Vaughan Williams, you couldn't like Elgar. Ludicrous, but true. Thank heavens that has gone today.

Symptomatic of the former English attitude to Mahler was the decision that his inclusion in the 'Master Musicians' series should be on a sharing basis—with Bruckner, of course! Each of these great figures now receives a volume to himself, but it would be remiss of me not to pay a tribute to my old friend Hans Redlich's book, which has made such a valuable contribution to a fuller understanding of both composers. He would surely have been delighted that J. M. Dent have now freed them from double harness.

Mahler is not entirely free of misunderstanding, though, even now. I believe that there is a tendency towards too strong an emphasis on supposed defects in his personality arising largely from inaccuracies and distortions in Alma Mahler's book and partly from amateurish dabbling in psychoanalysis. The result is that not only the man but the music is misrepresented, albeit from the best of motives. An artist might well consider that it is as irritating to be fashionable for the wrong reasons as it is to be unfashionable for the right ones. The portrait of 'Mahler, a suitable case for treatment' has been overdone.

I would like to acknowledge a very special debt of gratitude to Mr Renaud C. Bruce, of New York, who went to immense trouble on my behalf in research on Mahler's years in New York, and to Miss Carlotta Wilsen, of the New York Philharmonic Society, for all the assistance she gave him. For help in various ways I thank Mr and Mrs Henry Raynor, Mr Deryck Cooke, Mrs H. F. Riley, Mr Kenneth Thompson, Mr C. E. Meek, Assistant Chief Librarian of the City of New York Fire Department, Dr Wolfgang Stresemann, Intendant of the Berlin Philharmonic, Dr N. Campbell Brown, Dr D. U. Bloor, and Mrs A. Wragg.

I gratefully acknowledge permission to quote from Mahler's letters as published by John Murray Ltd in Alma Mahler's *Gustav Mahler: Memories and Letters* (enlarged edition, 1968) and I thank Universal Edition for permission to reproduce extracts from Mahler's published scores. In assembling illustrations I acknowledge help from Miss Anna Mahler, the Mansell Collection, the Austrian National Library, the State Library, Berlin, and Mr H. J. Nieman, of the Dutch branch of the Internationale Gustav Mahler Gesellschaft.

Sale, Cheshire. February 1974.   Michael Kennedy.

Contents

Illustrations

To Christopher Bishop

'A great example to all creative people is Jacob, who battles with God until He blesses him. God does not want to give me His blessing, either. Only through the fearful battles I have to fight to create my music do I receive His blessing in the end.'

GUSTAV MAHLER

1 The boy martyr

The music of Gustav Mahler is the bridge from the nineteenth century to the twentieth. His last seven major works were composed in the first decade of the twentieth century, which was also the last decade of his life; and while it is true that in his music we can hear the culmination of the Romantic tradition, it is equally true that in it we hear the music of the new epoch in composition which followed the overthrow of tonality. Nostalgia and prophecy, both are there, symbolic of Mahler as man and musician. Arnold Schoenberg summed it up in a letter he wrote to Mahler in 1909: 'I rank you with the classical composers; but as one who to me is still a *pioneer*.'

Of Mahler's great contemporaries—Richard Strauss, Jean Sibelius and Edward Elgar—none evoked from the succeeding generation of composers the kind of admiration which was accorded to Mahler by Schoenberg, Berg and Webern—not admiration based solely on 'liking' his music but on regarding him as a teacher, a source, a fellow radical. Nor was this true only of their generation. The *avant-garde* leader of a later day, Karlheinz Stockhausen, has acknowledged a debt to Mahler; and so have composers of more conservative outlook, Shostakovich and Britten. Likewise conductors. Bruno Walter, whose musical sympathies did not lie with the progressives, found in Mahler the heir of Schubert and Bruckner. Pierre Boulez, like Mahler a composer-conductor, is a devoted Mahlerian; and Sir John Barbirolli, for whom the music of Boulez and his followers held little appeal, found in the works of Mahler the novelty and adventure without which creative and executive artists become stagnant. Even more important, audiences throughout the world hear in Mahler's music a modern voice which speaks to them in terms they can understand. They recognize that it is a troubled voice, the voice of a man beset by doubts and fears which have always nagged at mankind's consciousness but which the dwellers in the second half of the twentieth century sometimes seem conceitedly to imagine are exclusively theirs. It is music of exultation and hope, of fatalism and optimism, of anguished questioning and universal affirmation, of emotional intensity and intellectual detachment, worldly-wise and world-weary. This is the essence of Mahler; largely because of it—and notwithstanding Schoenberg, Stravinsky and Debussy—the proposition is tenable that it is Mahler who has had the most potent widespread influence on twentieth-century music.

Mahler's life and work must be viewed in the light of three of his own sayings:

'I am thrice homeless, as a native of Bohemia in Austria, as an Austrian among Germans and as a Jew throughout all the world. Everywhere an intruder, never welcomed.'

'My beliefs? I am a musician. That says everything.'

'The symphony is the world! The symphony must embrace everything.'

Although Mahler and his work have at last come into their own, both are still widely regarded as 'neurotic', 'self-indulgent' and 'decadent'. None of these epithets is accurate. None is deserved.

In the nineteenth century large Jewish colonies lived uneasily in Bohemia and Moravia, then crown lands in the Austrian Empire ruled by Franz Joseph I. At Kališt, Bohemia, in 1827 Bernard Mahler was born. A coachman who became the proprietor of a small drink-shop or off-licence, Bernard married in 1857 Marie Hermann, the twenty-year-old daughter of a soap-maker. Marie married 'on the rebound'. She did not love Bernard and indeed they were remarkably ill matched, he coarse, virile, uninhibited, ambitious and with intellectual pretensions, she lame from birth and conscious of having married 'beneath her'. Fourteen children were born from this misalliance. The first, a son, Isidor (b. 1858), died in early infancy from some mishap. In 1860 on 7th July Gustav was born. Of the twelve subsequent children, six died in childhood from diphtheria or similar scourges. Six others of whom we shall hear further were Ernst (b. 1861), Leopoldine (b. 1863), Alois (b. 1867), Justine (b. 1868), Otto (b. 1873) and Emma (b. 1875). Marie Mahler was forty-two when her fourteenth child, Konrad, was born in 1879. He lived twenty-one months.

The marks of his childhood stayed with Gustav all his life. Perhaps out of sympathetic imitation of his mother's limp, he manifested as a child the peculiar gait—a change of pace every three or four steps—which was often the first thing people noticed about him, even in New York in his last years. Mahler's wife Alma wrote [1] that he 'dreamed his way through family life and childhood. He saw nothing of the unending tortures his mother had to endure from the brutality of his father'. This is inaccurate. In August 1910 Mahler consulted Sigmund Freud, the psychoanalyst, and in the course of their talk related this incident, which was recounted by Freud in a letter to Marie Bonaparte in 1925:

His father, apparently a brutal person, treated his wife very badly, and when Mahler was a young boy there was a specially painful scene between them. It became quite unbearable to the boy, who rushed away from the house. At that moment, however, a hurdy-gurdy in the street was grinding out the popular Viennese air *O, du lieber Augustin*. In Mahler's opinion the conjunction of high tragedy and light amusement was from then on inextricably fixed in his mind, and the one mood inevitably brought the other with it.[2]

[1] Alma Mahler, *Gustav Mahler, Memories and Letters* (2nd ed., 1968), p. 7.
[2] Ernest Jones, *Sigmund Freud: Life and Work, Vol. II* (1955), p. 89.

It would be wise not to be too ingenuous about this piece of Mahlerian self-analysis, especially the conclusion which Freud said Mahler drew from it. He 'suddenly said that now he understood why his music had always been prevented from achieving the highest rank through the noblest passages, those inspired by the most profound emotions, being spoilt by the intrusion of some commonplace melody'.[3] It is all too pat, like a film-scenario simplification of an interview between Freud and Mahler. Of course Freud diagnosed a mother-fixation (and a father-fixation in Alma) and of course Mahler dredged this incident from his memory. But one suspects an element of scepticism in Mahler's approach to the encounter. It is difficult to believe that he really thought the juxtaposition of pathos and bathos 'spoiled' his works: many of the finest and most effective passages in his symphonies are occasioned by it, as he must have known. His model in this respect could well have been Schubert's Octet.

The roots of Mahler's virtues and failings both as man and composer may be found in other aspects of his childhood background. First, the consciousness of being a Jew. Even though in the Austria of Mahler's youth the attitude to Jews was reasonably liberal, they were still left in little doubt that they were 'outsiders', subject to frequent outbursts of anti-Semitic prejudice, tolerated by some but openly derided by the German minority. When Mahler was born in 1860 there were still restrictions on their movements, although these were lifted during that year, enabling Bernard Mahler to move his business in December to Jihlava (Iglau). The inevitable consequence of their treatment was that some members of the Jewish communities became aggressively self-assertive. Bernard Mahler, who seems to have been a typical *petit bourgeois*, took a leading part in the life of the Jewish community, and Gustav received an orthodox Jewish education. In later life, as we shall see, he became a Roman

[3] Ernest Jones, *Sigmund Freud*, op. cit.

Catholic for political reasons, but he never denied his Jewish origin (not that he could easily have done so, because his appearance betrayed him). He disliked jokes about Jews, but asked his wife to warn him when he gesticulated too much because he thought it 'ill bred'.

Secondly, there was *Des Knaben Wunderhorn (Youth's Magic Horn)*. This famous anthology of German folk-poetry was published in two volumes between 1805 and 1808 by Achim von Arnim and Clemens Brentano. To an English mind it suggests an anachronistic mixture of Grimm fairy-tales and A. E. Housman—one might call it *A Salzkammergut Lad*. In these poems, dead soldiers answer a roll-call, girls try to lure sentries from their duty, St Anthony preaches to the fishes, drummer-boys go to the gallows, the cuckoo and the nightingale have a song contest with the donkey as judge. Always there are the symbols of night, of lost love, of the beauties of nature, of sudden death and trumpet-calls. It is sometimes said that Mahler discovered the *Wunderhorn* poems in his twenties, but Ida Dehmel, widow of the poet Richard Dehmel, recorded a conversation with Mahler in 1905 from which she learned that 'from earliest childhood his relationship to the book had been particularly close'.[4] Everything points to this being true. The book's spell would have been intensified in the boy's mind by the associations of its atmosphere with the reality of living near an army barracks and loitering there to listen to the bugles and the bands. From Slavonic servant girls he learned folk-tunes which, at the age of four, he could play on an accordion or concertina.

Musical talent, as is apparent from the foregoing, early showed itself in Mahler. At the age of five or six, on a visit to his maternal grandparents, he was found in the attic, strumming on an old pianoforte. Bernard Mahler, impelled by desire for cultural improvement and by the not unworthy ambition that his

4 See Alma Mahler's *Gustav Mahler*, op. cit., p. 93.

children should succeed where he had failed, decided that Gustav's future lay in music. Within three years the boy had progressed so well that he could give pianoforte lessons to another boy. On 13th October 1870, when he was ten, he gave a public recital in Jihlava. In the winter of 1870–1 he was sent by his father to study at the Gymnasium in Prague and to continue pianoforte lessons in the home of the Grünfeld family, who owned a music shop. Here he was ill treated, his shoes and clothes were taken from him and others given to him to wear, his diet was near-starvation. Years later he told his wife: 'I accepted it as a matter of course.' All accounts of Mahler's boyhood mention his extreme passivity in the face of suffering and his dreaminess, as if he was oblivious of the anger and cruelty directed towards him, although the likely explanation is that he was deliberately suppressing their effect on him. Asked what he would like to be 'when he grew up', Gustav replied: 'A martyr.'

Eventually his father heard of the conditions at the Grünfeld house and fetched Gustav home, but not before the boy had witnessed, involuntarily, a crude love passage between one of the Grünfeld sons and a maidservant. Thinking the girl needed rescuing, he went across to her but was violently abused by both lovers. At home in Jihlava Gustav's music lessons continued. He also read widely and deeply—where literature was concerned he was always an intellectual—and perhaps he had his father to thank for this too, for Bernard boasted of having a library. In any case his taste for philosophical and religious controversy was typically Jewish. During 1874 he passed through the miserable experience of his thirteen-year-old brother Ernst's long fatal illness, hydrocardia. 'For months he scarcely left his bedside and never tired of telling him stories,' Alma relates.[5] In the spring of 1875, on the prompting of an estate manager, who heard Gustav play Beethoven's *Les Adieux* sonata, Mahler's father took him to

[5] Alma Mahler, *Gustav Mahler*, op. cit., p. 7.

Vienna to play to Julius Epstein (1832–1926), professor of the pianoforte at the Conservatory. Epstein was 'struck by a remarkable look in the boy's face'. After hearing Gustav play a few bars he said: 'He is a born musician ... I cannot possibly be wrong.'[6]

[6] Paul Stefan, *Gustav Mahler, a study of his personality and work* (1931), p. 13. Some accounts say that Mahler was first taken to Epstein by the estate manager, whose name was Gustav Schwarz.

2 Bruckner's disciples

Mahler entered the Vienna Conservatory in September 1875. The director since 1851 had been Joseph Hellmesberger, violinist, leader of a celebrated string quartet, conductor, and anti-Semite. He was forty-seven. Mahler's teachers were Julius Epstein for pianoforte, Robert Fuchs (1847–1925)—who had only recently joined the staff—for harmony, and Franz Krenn (1816–97) for composition. Fuchs told Alma Mahler years afterwards: 'Mahler always played truant and yet there was nothing he couldn't do.' That he was already a composer of songs may be deduced from the fact that his fellow students spoke of him as 'another Schubert'. He also continued privately with his general education, for which he paid by giving pianoforte lessons.

These fellow students are of more interest than the professors, notably Hugo Wolf, Hans Rott (like Wolf, he died insane), and Rudolf Krzyzanowski, who was Mahler's closest friend. Together they shared poverty. Mahler was slightly more fortunate than the others: he had the income from his teaching (using some of it on one occasion to pay for the hire of Wolf's pianoforte) and his parents sent him parcels of food and clothing. Even so he was very poor and in 1876 applied to the Conservatory, with Epstein's support, to be excused his fees. Epstein, in fact, paid a half fee for Mahler from 1876–7 onwards and found him pianoforte pupils, including his son Richard. Mahler's impulsive industriousness was evident even then and in 1880 it caused a rift with Wolf which foreshadowed the tragedy to follow. Wolf confided his wish to compose a fairy-tale opera and, in discussion with Mahler, chose *Rübezahl*. Mahler began work on the libretto and completed it within a few hours. He showed it to Wolf, who had also made a start. Wolf was so offended that he abandoned the scheme. Mahler's libretto still exists.

There was another—and important—common factor binding these young men: their admiration for, leading to friendship with, Anton Bruckner, who at this date was fifty-two. He went to concerts with them, preferring to stand in their company than to sit in the comfort of a box. Rott was a special favourite and it was probably through him that Mahler met Bruckner. One may imagine with what excitement the youths listened to his account of his journey to Bayreuth in 1876 for the first cycle of Wagner's *Der Ring*. Mahler enrolled for various courses at the university so that he could attend Bruckner's lectures, but instead of attending philosophy lectures he 'industriously visited the Vienna Woods'.

'I was never a pupil of Bruckner,' Mahler wrote.[1] 'Everyone thinks I studied with him because in my student days in Vienna I was so often in his company and was reckoned among his first disciples. Bruckner's happy disposition and his childlike, trusting nature made our relationship one of open friendship. Naturally the realization and understanding of his ideals which I then arrived at cannot have been without influence upon my development as artist and man.'

On 16th December 1877 the second version of Bruckner's Third Symphony was performed by the Vienna Philharmonic Orchestra, who had refused to play the first version three years earlier. The occasion was a disaster, but the unfortunate Bruckner was comforted by the enthusiasm of the two seventeen-year-olds, Mahler and Rudolf Krzyzanowski. To them he entrusted the task of making a pianoforte-duet arrangement of the symphony, under Epstein's supervision. This was published by Rättig in 1878, and Bruckner was so pleased that he gave his

[1] Gabriel Engel, *Gustav Mahler, Song-Symphonist* (New York, 1932), p. 21.

manuscript of the second version to Mahler. (This manuscript score, which lacked the finale, was bought by the Austrian Government from Alma Mahler in 1948.)

Mahler left the Conservatory, having gained his diploma, at the end of the summer term in July 1878. He had had a successful sojourn there: prizes for piano playing (Schubert's A minor sonata) in 1875–6 and 1876–7, and the composition prize in 1876–7 for the first movement of a pianoforte quintet. On his last day at the Conservatory the prize-winning *scherzo* of another Mahler pianoforte quintet was played. He had had frustrations too, including the refusal by Hellmesberger to continue rehearsing the students' orchestra in a symphony he had written [2] because 'your parts are full of mistakes'.

The Vienna of Mahler's impressionable youth had just emerged from the period in which it had become, both in appearance and in fact, a great administrative imperial capital. Its bourgeois atmosphere was a compound of sophistication and sentimentality. In its close-knit society, intrigues flourished and artists were worshipped or detested, such was the overriding interest in music, theatre and the graphic arts. The name and work of Richard Wagner still evoked passions and prejudices of the most violent, disproportionate and humourless kind, splitting families, affecting politics, determining lives. To the young he was a god; to the middle aged and elderly he was antichrist. No one could be neutral. In Mahler's first term at the Conservatory, in the winter of 1875, Wagner went to Vienna to supervise productions of *Tannhäuser* and *Lohengrin*. His visit was the major topic of conversation, and of course his antagonists, led by the critic Eduard Hanslick, went into action. The fanatical devotion to Wagner which these performances generated in Hugo Wolf is well known.[3] Mahler too may be presumed to have been equally spellbound.

[2] Presumed to be one of two symphonies of this period.
[3] See Frank Walker, *Hugo Wolf* (London, 2nd ed., 1968), pp. 26–33.

Yet we can also perceive what effect this sort of episode must have had on his sensitive and solitary nature. A Jew with his family background would inevitably feel isolated in Viennese society; add to this that he now saw what senseless and bitter hatred could be directed against creative geniuses like Wagner and Bruckner. After all, he had himself seen Hellmesberger, the Conservatory director, laughing and jeering at Bruckner's Third Symphony. He saw too with what simple faith Bruckner was able to combat the malevolence of his detractors and how his music remained unaffected by bitterness. He saw, with the fierce vision of adolescence, the depths of human suffering experienced within his own family: the deaths of Ernst and the other children, the unhinged behaviour of two of his brothers and of some of his friends, such as Rott, the misery of his parents. Imagine all these impressions crowding into a mind already striving to express itself in music and one has an epitome of the violent contrast in his spiritual outlook on mankind: regarding it in one light as squalid and base, in another as a doomed aspirant for redemption —perhaps for resurrection, even—infinitely deserving of compassion. What could he really believe? There is the crux of his lifelong inner conflict and tension, so obviously reflected in his music. No wonder that, like so many other doubters, he took comfort from the one unchanging elemental, the beauty of nature, a consolation for even the inescapable fact of one's own mortality. No wonder we find him, at the age of eighteen, writing to his friend Joseph Steiner (about whom little is known and who disappeared from Mahler's life in 1879) in these romanticized but significant terms:

O my beloved earth, when, oh when will you take the forsaken one to your breast? Behold, mankind has banished him from itself, and he flees from its cold and heartless bosom to you, to you! Oh care for the lonely one, the restless one, Universal Mother!

The forsaken one—the martyr! In that outburst is a forerunner of the poetic sentiments which were to inspire his master-piece, *Das Lied von der Erde*, over twenty-five years later: 'Whither I go? . . . I seek rest for my lonely heart! . . . the dear earth everywhere grows green again.' To all this add, as a further facet of his complex personality, that Mahler was subject, like many creative artists, to periods of sudden melancholia. As he wrote in 1894:

> I am in the grip of the past, of all that I have lost, of the present with its loneliness. . . . You know I have had these moods from my youth. I often used to get these fits of melancholy when I was in the midst of my friends. There was *no one* with whom I could have anything in common, no one with whom I could share my experiences, my visions, my hopes.

This is the characteristic complaint of the artist, yet another indication of the isolation he felt simply because he was a creator. Elgar, another poor boy who made good, whom Mahler resembles in several other respects, was also deeply conscious of this loneliness and complained strongly that 'no one wanted him'. But to interpret Mahler's adolescent letter to Steiner as symptomatic of a 'death-wish' is to go too far. It is easy to speak of men having a 'death-wish', but not easy to prove it. There is no doubt that Mahler, in common with the rest of mankind, thought a lot about death and was eventually forced to face the comparative brevity of his own life, but his music accepts death as a reality and is often filled with joyful affirmation of life and of the world's beauty. It is true he also wrote to Steiner: 'The highest ecstasy of the most joyous zest for living and the most burning desire for death: these two reign alternately within my heart,' but one must allow for the violent extremes of adolescence and remember the compensating resilience of youth.

After leaving the Conservatory in 1878 Mahler returned to Jihlava in the late summer to pass his matriculation. He earned a precarious living by giving pianoforte lessons, but his preoccupation was with his compositions. While at the Conservatory he had composed part of a pianoforte quartet, and had written a violin sonata and a pianoforte quintet, both of which were played at Jihlava on 12th September 1876. In 1875–6 he worked on an opera, *Herzog Ernst von Schwaben*, for which his friend Steiner provided the libretto, but laid it aside and started work on a dramatic cantata, *Das klagende Lied*. For the latter he first wrote the poem himself, completing it in March 1878. After his holiday at home in 1878 he returned to Vienna in the autumn ostensibly to attend lectures at the university. He earned money from teaching the pianoforte, and shared lodgings and poverty with Hugo Wolf and Rudolf Krzyzanowski. In the summer of 1879 he went as piano-tutor to a family in Hungary, returning to Vienna in September, after a holiday in Jihlava, where a romance with the postmaster's daughter, Josephine Poisl, bore musical fruit in three songs.

Throughout this period he was at work on the music for *Das klagende Lied*. This typical piece of German fairy-tale romanticism was the first fruit of the influence of *Des Knaben Wunderhorn*. He completed the full score on 1st November 1880. On that day he wrote to Emil Freund: 'My fairy-tale is at last finished—a real child of sorrow at which I've worked for over a year. As a result it's in good shape. My next aim is to bring about its performance by any means I can think of.' In this aim he failed. He entered it in 1881 for the Beethoven Prize of 500 gulden instituted in 1875 by the Gesellschaft der Musikfreunde and open to present and past Conservatory students. The jury included Brahms, Hans Richter and Carl Goldmark, and they rejected Mahler's cantata.

3 On the treadmill

Mahler said in later life that if he had won the Beethoven Prize he could have avoided 'this treadmill of the theatre', by which he meant conducting opera. He was romanticizing. He had begun his career as a conductor before he even finished *Das klagende Lied*. He had been given a post at the health resort of Hall, Upper Austria, in the summer of 1880 to conduct musical comedies and to perform such chores as tidying the pit after the performance. What remains unexplained is why he was advised to try conducting when he had hitherto shown no inclination in that direction. According to Paul Stefan,[1] the publisher Rättig advised Mahler to see an agent. Through this agent the Hall engagement was offered and accepted against the advice of Mahler's parents but on the advice of Epstein, his mentor and pianoforte teacher. Up to this point it might have been expected that Mahler would become a concert pianist. Accounts of his playing indicate that it was exceptionally compelling, especially of Beethoven and Bach. Yet after about 1880, except for chamber music for pleasure and playing through what he had written, he confined his playing to occasional appearances as accompanist in recitals of his songs. Otto Klemperer heard him in Berlin in 1906 as accompanist to the Dutch baritone Johannes Meschaert.[2]

After the summer at Hall—the theatre was a tiny wooden con-

[1] P. Stefan, *Gustav Mahler*, op. cit., p. 20.
[2] A Welte piano-roll recording, made in Germany, of Mahler playing the finale of his Fourth Symphony is included in Bernstein's box-set of the symphonies (CBS 77508).

struction, seating about 200, unfit for use in wet weather—
Mahler returned to Vienna and his pianoforte pupils. He finished
Das klagende Lied and began an opera on the classical subject
Die Argonauten. During 1881 he went to Laibach (now Ljub-
ljana) for a six-month season at the Landestheater, conducting
such operas as *Il Trovatore*, *Faust*, *Die Zauberflöte*, *Martha*
and *Freischütz*. Back in Vienna he worked on another opera,
never completed, *Rübezahl* (the cause of his rift with Wolf over
the libretto), and on a *Nordic Symphony*. In 1882, on 19th September, his home town of Jihlava saw him in action as a conductor
when he conducted Suppé's operetta *Boccaccio* there. These early
operatic experiences were invaluable. He learned how to cope
with inadequacies and how to adapt. For three months from
January to March 1883 he conducted at Olmütz (Olomouc), also
in Moravia, where under primitive conditions he directed works
by Meyerbeer, Verdi and Méhul (*Joseph*). News of his success with
Bizet's *Carmen*, which had first been produced only eight years
earlier, reached Treiber, the principal conductor of opera at the
Royal Prussian Court Theatre at Cassel. A stage director who
had watched him at Olmütz commended his ability to obtain
good results from poor material. An invitation followed to
Mahler to become second conductor at Cassel in the autumn of
1883. There he quickly became disillusioned because Treiber
insisted on confining him to comic operas by lesser composers.
In January 1884 he wrote to Hans von Bülow asking if he could
become personal assistant and pupil. Bülow sent the letter to
Treiber.

Already the fanatical zeal which characterized his genius as a
conductor was evident. He was, as we should now say, 'a
natural'. To those who shared his ideals he seemed like the
answer to their prayers; to the others—in his opinion fools, and
he suffered them much less than gladly—he was the reverse.
Friedrich Eckstein, who had been at the Conservatory with him,
described him at this period:

Already in the curiously wagging manner of his gait, his unusual irritability manifested itself. His tense and intellectual face, thin and extremely mobile, was framed by a full brown beard; his speech was pointed, with a strongly Austrian intonation. He invariably carried a parcel of books and music under his arm.

By now the pattern of Mahler's life was established—conductor and composer, one activity rivalling but fertilizing the other. He had one of those dual natures which need to be at full stretch, to be in perpetual conflict between one set of pressures and the other. To the scholar Guido Adler he analysed himself correctly: 'I need *practical* exercise for my musical ability to counterbalance the enormous creative activity that goes on within.' The warring elements in Mahler—the mystic and the man of action, the composer and the conductor—were the catalyst for his genius. Although he sometimes complained about his conducting 'crushing his soul' it became a necessity for him, if only because it enabled him to keep in intimate touch with the practical mechanics of his art.

At Cassel Mahler had another affair of the heart, with a singer Johanna Richter. It came to an unhappy end, but it inspired him to begin a song-cycle in November 1884. 'I have written a cycle of songs, six for the present, all of which are dedicated to her,' he wrote to his friend Löhr after he had completed the song-cycle in December 1884. 'The songs are conceived to suggest a wayfarer who has met with adversity setting out into the world and wandering on in solitude.' He had written the verses too, and the song-cycle, containing four songs, not six, has come down to us as *Lieder eines fahrenden Gesellen* (*Songs of a Wayfarer*), his first masterpiece.

During the early part of 1884 he wrote incidental music for several performances given in June of J. V. von Scheffel's then popular pageant play, *Der Trompeter von Säkkingen.* As will be seen later, this was to be important in relation to the First Symphony on which he also began to work at this time. Because of his dissatisfaction with Cassel (where it was felt that he had lost interest) he went to Dresden, ostensibly to hear *Tristan und Isolde* for the first time but also to call on the conductor Ernst von Schuch, in the hope of obtaining a post. He failed, but left Cassel on 1st July 1885, after being invited for (but later cancelling) a month's trial at Leipzig. An engagement as second conductor for 1886–7 followed. To cover the intervening year he went to the Deutsches Landestheater, Prague, as second conductor to Slansky. He did so well with Cherubini's *Les deux journées* that the director, Angelo Neumann, the Wagnerian proselyte, entrusted to him *Rienzi, Meistersinger, Das Rheingold* and *Die Walküre* in addition to *Fidelio*, Gluck's *Iphigénie en Aulide* and, ironically, Viktor Nessler's opera based on *Der Trompeter von Säkkingen.* While in Prague he had a love-affair with another singer, Betty Frank, the first to perform his songs in public.

He took up the Leipzig post in August 1886. The director was Max Stägemann and the principal conductor since 1882 had been Arthur Nikisch, who was five years older than Mahler. Nikisch at this time had a long illness and Mahler stepped into the breach, his Wagner performances becoming both controversial and popular. In Leipzig he met Hauptmann von Weber, grandson of the composer, who invited him to inspect the fragmentary notes and sketches of Weber's comic opera, *Die drei Pintos*, and try to complete or reconstruct it. This Mahler did, thereby coming much into contact with Marion Mathilda von Weber, the Hauptmann's wife, with whom he fell in love, although he was her junior in years (and by now clean-shaven). The opera was staged, with Mahler conducting, on 20th January 1888 and was successful. Other performances followed elsewhere, including Vienna.

Friction developed with Nikisch and Stägemann, leading to Mahler's resignation from Leipzig in May 1888. He applied for conducting posts in Carlsruhe, Budapest and Hamburg, but his reputation among opera intendants had suffered because of his affairs with singers and with Frau Weber, and because of his fiery artistic temperament. Eventually Franz von Beniczky, director of the Budapest Opera, offered him a ten-year contract as chief conductor from October 1888. He was given a free hand to reorganize the Opera and to rescue it from near-bankruptcy, both financial and artistic. This was his first chance really to display his genius not only as a conductor but as an administrator. He determined, although he could not speak Hungarian, to create a national company unhampered by imported and expensive stars.

He succeeded, when in some physical pain and at a time of personal strain. Within three months he had staged *Das Rheingold* in Hungarian, quickly following it with *Die Walküre*, but his plan to complete *Der Ring* failed. Word of his prowess spread, audiences increased and the company made a profit. (It should not be forgotten when there is discussion of Mahler's so-called 'unbalanced' nature that to run opera companies as he did in Budapest, Hamburg and Vienna requires exceptional administrative acumen.) On 18th February 1889 his father died at the age of sixty-one. Whatever his feelings, Mahler owed his musical education to Bernard's encouragement, and not every young musician can say that. He had made no attempt to break with his family, returning regularly to Jihlava for summer holidays even when he knew that his parents' unhappiness and increasing ill health would depress and aggravate him. 'I myself, so hard and cruel to them—and yet I can't help it, and torment them to distraction,' he had written to Friedrich Löhr in the summer of 1883.[3] It is possible that he was prepared to put up with this emotional stress for the sake of the walks in the countryside near his home. The necessity for regular contact with the beauties of nature was as strong for Mahler as it was for Beethoven, and a powerful stimulus to composition, as is obvious from his music, in which birdsong and the sound of village festivities are frequent

[3] *Gustav Mahler Briefe*, ed. Alma Mahler (Berlin, 1924), p. 22.

features. When he was walking with his friend, the violinist Natalie Bauer-Lechner (1858–1921), they heard a medley of village sounds—fairground booths, merry-go-rounds, military marches. 'Do you hear it?' Mahler exclaimed. 'That is polyphony. That's where I got it from'.[4]

In July of 1889 he had a painful operation for haemorrhoids. In 1889 too, on 11th October, his mother died, aged fifty-two. So Gustav was now head of the family, responsible for his surviving two sisters and two brothers. The next oldest to him, his sister Leopoldine, had also died in 1889 from a brain tumour. His ne'er-do-well brother Alois was now twenty-two. His sister Justine, who had nursed their dying mother, was nearly twenty-one, a neurotic girl with a vivid imagination. Otto, a talented composer and Mahler's favourite, was fifteen. The youngest, at thirteen, was Emma. Mahler sold his parents' business, gave his share of the proceeds to his sisters and ordered his brothers to do likewise, much to their chagrin. He took Justine to Budapest to keep house for him. From this time their particularly intense relationship developed. It was with all this on his mind that he conducted in Budapest on 20th November 1889 the first performance of what we know as the First Symphony but which was then described as a Symphonic Poem in five movements. It was coldly received.

Mahler soon realized that the favourable atmosphere at the Budapest Royal Opera House would not last and he began to put out feelers elsewhere, in particular to Hamburg. In December 1890 he conducted a *Don Giovanni* which Brahms declared to be the best he had heard; in the next month Beniczky resigned and was succeeded by the one-armed Count Zichy, a fanatical nationalist. Zichy clashed with Mahler by interfering where Beniczky had given a free hand. After an especially violent quarrel Mahler arrived at the opera house to find himself locked out. He was, in

[4] N. Bauer-Lechner, *Erinnerungen an Gustav Mahler* (Leipzig, 1923), p. 147.

effect, dismissed, but insisted upon the large sum of 25,000 florins as compensation for the breaking of his contract. He formally resigned on 14th March and used some of the money for a large flat for his brothers and sisters in Vienna. Meanwhile he had received a telegram from Bernhard Pollini,[5] director of the Hamburg Municipal Theatre, offering him the post of chief conductor. He took up the post on 29th March and was to remain in it for six important years.

[5] Pollini was born Bernhard Pohl and had been a tenor. He had been director at Hamburg since 1873. Wits called him 'Monopollini'.

4 Hamburg's Pygmalion

Hamburg has a long and honourable musical tradition. When Mahler arrived there the city's symphony concerts were in the charge of another great conductor, Hans von Bülow. Within the first few days of his régime Mahler conducted *Siegfried*. Bülow attended the performance and wrote to his daughter Daniela on 24th April 1891: 'Hamburg has now acquired a simply first-rate opera conductor in Mr Gustav Mahler . . . who in my opinion equals the very best conductors (Mottl, Richter etc.). . . . Recently I heard *Siegfried* under his direction. . . . Without an orchestral rehearsal, he compelled the musical rabble to dance to his tune.' Mahler quickly began to infuse into Hamburg the same zeal for artistic perfection which had marked his stay in Budapest. But now he had the advantage of an excellent orchestra and of gifted singers already under contract to the shrewd Pollini, among them the soprano Katharina Klafsky, a great Leonora in *Fidelio*, whose husband, Otto Lohse, was second conductor; the tenors Max Alvary and Julius Lieban, and the contralto Ernestine Schumann-Heink. The operas of Mozart and Wagner—and Beethoven's *Fidelio*—were the foundation of his work, but he lost no chance to introduce new works during his tenure— Puccini's *Manon Lescaut*, Verdi's *Falstaff*, Humperdinck's *Hänsel und Gretel*—and unfamiliar ones such as Tchaikovsky's *Eugen Onegin* (with the composer present). Smetana's *Dalibor* and *The Bartered Bride* and Bizet's *Djamileh*. The public, he told his sister, 'adores me, but Pollini is "dumb as an ox"'.

In June and July 1892 Mahler visited London for the only time in his life. Sir Augustus Harris, manager of Covent Garden, planned to stage *Der Ring* for the first time at the Royal Opera House [1] and through his friend Pollini engaged a German cast, the nucleus of which was the Hamburg company with the addition of two Bayreuth stars, Rosa Sucher (as Isolde) and Theodor Reichmann, noted for his Sachs. Harris wanted Richter, since 1877 a regular visitor to London, as conductor but he was busy in Vienna and Pollini urged Mahler instead. With typical thoroughness Mahler at once began to learn English, practising it on walks with a Hamburg friend, the physicist Arnold Berliner. From 69 Torrington Square he wrote to Berliner: 'I found the circumstances of orchestra here bader than thought and the cast better than hoped. . . . I make greater progress in English as you can observe.'

The performances of *Tristan und Isolde* and *Fidelio*—which were both staged at the Theatre Royal, Drury Lane—were a revelation to London audiences. Among those who heard *Tristan* was a twenty-two-year-old conductor at the beginning of his career, Henry J. Wood (he met Mahler), and a nineteen-year-old composition student at the Royal College of Music, Ralph Vaughan Williams, who was so moved that he told his teacher, Hubert Parry, he was unable to sleep for two nights. The critics were far from unanimous about *Fidelio* (its first performance in German in England), finding Mahler's reading 'unconventional'. Mahler wrote to Berliner: 'All the same, the public absolved me from my blasphemy with a regular *hurricane* of applause—in fact, they overwhelm me with endless tokens of sympathy. I've got to go before the curtain literally after *every act*—the whole house yells "Mahler" till I appear.' By this time he performed the *Leonora No. 3* overture between the two scenes

[1] The cycle had only once before been performed in London, in 1882 at Her Majesty's under Angelo Neumann. It was given under Mahler out of sequence, thus: *Siegfried* (3), *Das Rheingold* (1), *Die Walküre* (2), *Götterdämmerung* (4).

of Act II instead of between the acts. He first began this practice in Hamburg in April 1891, and continued it thereafter, although it is said to have been inaugurated by Mottl [2] at Carlsruhe. No doubt there are other candidates.

The transformation Mahler wrought at Hamburg can be gauged from the continuing admiration of Bülow. He sent Mahler a laurel wreath inscribed 'To the Pygmalion of the Hamburg Opera'. When Bülow's health failed Mahler deputized for him, the first occasion being on 12th December 1892. After Bülow's death in Cairo on 12th February 1894 Mahler succeeded him and thus became all-powerful in Hamburg. Bülow's admiration did not extend to Mahler's music. In September 1891 Mahler played to him the first movement of a symphony (No. 2) he had been writing for several years. Bülow did not like it—it made *Tristan* sound like a Haydn symphony by comparison, he said. He refused also to conduct some of Mahler's early songs with orchestra; they were 'far too strange'. Ironically, it was Bülow's funeral service which provided Mahler with the inspiration he was seeking to finish the Second Symphony. He was so impressed by Klopstock's hymn *Auferstehen* (Resurrection) that he incorporated it into the finale.

It is at this period of Mahler's life, when the demands of running a profitable opera company and his increasing success as a concert-hall conductor intensified, that he began to concentrate his composing into the duration of a summer holiday. Wryly, he described himself as 'der Sommerkomponist', the 'summer-composer'. As he put it in a letter to the critic and composer Max Marschalk in December 1896:

A man who is chained to the galleys of the theatre cannot manage to write as much music as the concert matadors of the day. He can only

[2] Felix Mottl (1856–1911) was conductor of the Carlsruhe Opera from 1881 to 1903, when he went to Munich. He was noted for his Wagner and Berlioz interpretations. He orchestrated Wagner's *Five Wesendonk Songs*.

write on red-letter days. On these occasions all his emotional experiences concentrate themselves into one work. I am constitutionally unable to do anything but pour body and soul into each new work.

From 1893 he spent his summers at Steinbach-am-Attersee, near Salzburg. During his first stay he revised the Symphonic Poem which had been such a failure in Budapest and Hamburg. He now called it a symphony, with the subtitle *Titan*, a homage to the novel by Jean Paul Richter. The revised score was performed at the Weimar Festival on 29th June 1894. Mahler described the result to Arnold Berliner:

My symphony was greeted with unbounded enthusiasm on one side and furious opposition on the other. Opinions were aired in the streets and drawing-rooms in a most edifying manner. For 'when the dogs begin to bark, we know we're on the way!' Of course, I was the winner (in my estimation, though scarcely in anyone else's).

Among those who read the hostile critical notices of this performance, especially of the movement called *Funeral March in the manner of Callot*, was a Jewish musician of seventeen, Bruno Schlesinger. He was fascinated by the idea of this work and determined somehow to work under its composer. So, a few months later, he obtained a post at Hamburg as coach and chorus-master. He is known to posterity by the name he adopted a few years later: Bruno Walter. Through Walter's eyes we see Mahler as he was then—midway through his Hamburg period and approaching his thirty-fifth birthday, with more than two-thirds of his life already lived:[3]

Pale, thin, small of stature [not much over five feet], with longish features, the steep forehead framed by intensely black hair, remarkable

[3] The quoted passages from Bruno Walter which follow are from his *Gustav Mahler*, trans. J. Galston (London, 1937) and his *Theme and Variations*, trans. J. Galston (London, 1947).

eyes behind spectacles, lines of sorrow and of humour in the face which, when he spoke to others, would show the most astonishing change of expression—the very incarnation of that Kapellmeister Kreisler—interesting, demoniac, intimidating—as he would appear to the imagination of youthful readers of E. Th. A. Hoffman's fantastic tales.

Walter hero-worshipped Mahler thenceforward, but was not blind to his hero's faults or the manifestations of his autocratic behaviour.

Never before had I seen such an intense person, never dreamed that a terse word, a commanding gesture, and a will directed solely towards a certain goal, could frighten and alarm others and force them into blind obedience. . . . I was fascinated to observe how the same intensity, the same spiritual tenseness, that had previously filled his rehearsing, was now manifested in his conversation. The vehemence with which he objected when I said something that was unsatisfactory to him . . . his sudden submersion in pensive silence, the kind glance with which he would receive an understanding word on my part, an unexpected, convulsive expression of secret sorrow and, added to all this, the strange irregularity of his walk: his stamping of the feet, sudden halting, rushing ahead again—everything confirmed and strengthened the impression of demoniac obsession.

Walter mentions again in another passage this frequent sudden changing of Mahler's facial expression from cheerfulness to gloom 'as if he were reproaching himself for having thoughtlessly forgotten to remember something that was sad'. Alma mentions the same trait; and we can recognize its reflection in his music. In Mahler's symphonies, one may say, every silver lining has a cloud. He had a natural gaiety, but he attached importance to 'suffering'.

From Walter too we have a detailed account of Mahler's intellectual curiosity and literary tastes, and the brilliance of his conversation: he was also a good listener, except in uncongenial company, when he made no attempt to disguise his boredom, for he had cultivated few social graces. In Hamburg in 1894 his principal literary preoccupations were Dostoyevsky and Schopenhauer—one can readily imagine the appeal to Mahler of Schopenhauer's theory of a universal Will which generates suffering, so that the more we know the more we suffer. The novels of Jean Paul Richter, Sterne's *Tristram Shandy*, Cervantes's *Don Quixote*, the poetry of Hölderlin, Nietzsche's *Zarathustra* and, of course, Goethe were among his favourites. ('Goethe and apples are two things he cannot live without', a friend said of him.) His interest in the natural sciences was also keen. Berliner had high praise for the acuteness of his understanding of physics. Walter recalls, too, happy evenings of music-making when Mahler and he played pianoforte works for four hands by Mozart, Schubert, Schumann and Dvořák, with Mahler inventing words to Schubert's march melodies and singing them while playing, then laughing uncontrollably and relapsing into 'gloom and silence which nobody dared to disturb'. It must have been unnerving.

Mahler was at once touched and flattered by Walter's devotion and readiness to listen. 'Whence do we come? Whither does our road take us?' he said to his impressionable young disciple. 'Why am I made to feel that I am free while yet I am constrained within my personality as in a prison? What is the object of toil and sorrow? Will the meaning of life be revealed by death?' These fundamental questions were at the root of the enormous work, the Second ('Resurrection') Symphony for soloists, chorus and orchestra which he had completed at Steinbach on 25th July 1894. The three instrumental movements (Nos. 1, 2 and 3) were performed in Berlin by the Berlin Philharmonic Orchestra conducted by Mahler in March 1895. Later in the year, on 13th December, he conducted the symphony in full, again with the Berlin orchestra which, according to Walter, he engaged at his own expense in order to have sufficient rehearsals. The audience and performers were ecstatic about the work; the critics were divided. The performance might well have been disastrous because—an important point in considering his volatile personality—Mahler was a regular sufferer from violent attacks of migraine. One of these prostrated him on the afternoon of the concert and only by a superhuman effort of will did he control those vast forces that evening.

It is hardly surprising that there should have been a physical manifestation of the strain Mahler was under, not only because of the personal and practical stresses involved in bringing such a tremendous work to birth, but also because his much-loved brother Otto had shot himself on 6th February 1895. Otto was also a musician—'more gifted than I', said Mahler, who paid for him to attend Vienna Conservatory for four years—but he lacked the application which distinguished his older brother. Mahler found him posts as choirmaster in provincial towns but Otto never stayed long. He left a suicide note saying that life no longer pleased him, so he 'handed back his ticket'. So now Mahler sold the Vienna flat, took Justine and Emma to Hamburg and left the hapless Alois to his own devices, although he was ever ready with money to help him out of trouble. In later years he was to say bitterly to his wife: 'You are lucky. You were born with a silver spoon in your mouth. You can go your flowery way—no grim past, no family round your neck—but I have had to stagger on all my life with clods of earth weighing down my feet.' Mahler was conscientiously devoted to his family.

Nor was all right with the world at the Hamburg opera. In the spring of this fated 1895 Klafsky and her husband Lohse, the second conductor, broke their contracts and went to America.[4] Pollini invited Walter to take over Lohse's position and engaged the twenty-three-year-old soprano, Anna von Mildenburg, destined to become one of the greatest, as successor to Klafsky. Mahler fell in love with her, causing anguish to the jealously

[4] Klafsky died suddenly at the age of forty-one in Germany in September 1896, just after returning to the Hamburg Opera.

possessive Justine, and giving the gossips of Hamburg a field-day, for the liaison was considered scandalous. Mildenburg was to become a fixed star of his Vienna régime. Of more concern to Mahler was the growing strain with Pollini which led to his disenchantment with Hamburg. Walter says that Pollini's 'gloomy reserve' and Mahler's 'fiery impetuosity' were bound to clash eventually, but there was also the practical point that Mahler, always striving for perfection, was dissatisfied with the quality of the staging of the operas and held Pollini responsible for giving him an unimaginative stage-manager with whom to work. Also he was sighing for new worlds to conquer, in particular Vienna.[5]

There is no longer doubt that Mahler schemed for a post in Vienna, where Wilhelm Jahn had been director of the Imperial Court Opera since 1881 and Hans Richter principal conductor since 1875. In 1896 he applied to several opera houses, Berlin, Dresden and Munich among them, but Vienna was his goal. To this end he enlisted the influential support of Brahms, visiting him several times at Bad Ischl and Vienna. But there were two obstacles; the deep-seated and intensifying opposition to Jews holding such posts as the Vienna directorship, and the unwritten law that court posts of that kind were not available to non-Catholics. Mahler had never been a practising Jew and his religious tenets were far beyond dogma. If it was expedient that he should become a Catholic, a Catholic he would become; and he did so, on 23rd February 1897. (Alma records that he could not pass a church without going inside and that he loved the smell of incense—aesthetic rather than devotional reactions.)

He had asked Pollini to release him from his Hamburg contract early in 1897 before leaving in March for a successful series of concerts in Russia and elsewhere. On 17th February

[5] He was also 'disgusted by the unblushing commercialism of the town council': Ethel Smyth, *What Happened Next* (London, 1940), p. 46.

1897 he wrote to the critic Arthur Seidl about the Vienna post:

Between ourselves, the crisis can only be solved next autumn and it seems now as if the choice will be between Mottl and yours truly. To tell you the truth, I do not know whether I ought to take that particular post. It may so easily make me a stranger to my own musical aims. . . . However, I am a complete fatalist in this matter and try to forget about it and just let things work out.

Rumours that Mahler would be appointed began to circulate in Vienna and opposition was mobilized by Hans Richter and the second conductor, Nepomuk Fuchs. They found a staunch ally in Cosima Wagner. (Mahler, one of the greatest Wagner conductors, was never invited to conduct at Bayreuth.) But the Intendant of the Opera, Josef von Bezecny, was determined to capture Mahler, realizing that only a fanatic with up-to-date ideas and unswerving ideals could drag the opera from its complacent torpor. On 1st May Mahler was engaged as a Kapellmeister and on 11th May he conducted *Lohengrin* 'on trial'. The performance was a sensation; and on 13th July he was made deputy director to Jahn. Then, on 8th October, the announcement was made of his appointment as principal conductor and director, with almost unlimited powers, a salary of 24,000 kroner a year, gratuities and a pension.

As a conductor Mahler had now achieved the summit of his profession at the age of thirty-seven. Yet he of all people knew how the hour of triumph is often marred by sorrow or cruelty. His first weeks at the Vienna Opera were overshadowed by the tragic end of an old friendship. It is true that the coolness with Hugo Wolf had persisted since the *Rübezahl* libretto episode and that since that time they had met only once, at Bayreuth in 1883, and merely acknowledged each other curtly; nevertheless they shared old memories. Although each disliked the other's music, Wolf greatly admired Mahler's conducting. On 4th June 1897

Mahler undertook to consider producing Wolf's opera *Der Corregidor*. In September Wolf went to see Mahler at his office, where they had a violent argument when Mahler told him that the work would not be performed during the 1897–8 season. This was enough, alas, to unbalance Wolf's precarious mental stability. He announced to his friends that Mahler had been dismissed and that he was now director. It was the beginning of the end, which came on 22nd February 1903; a year later Mahler conducted *Der Corregidor* in both its revised and original versions. It was not a success.

There was no 'summer-composing' in 1897, but Mahler went to Vienna having completed his Third Symphony at Steinbach in the summer of 1896, the year in which he had conducted the First Symphony in Berlin, preceding it with the first performance of his song-cycle *Lieder eines fahrenden Gesellen*. At Steinbach, amid the beauty of the Salzkammergut, he played the new six-movement symphony—'A Summer Morning's Dream'—to Bruno Walter. 'The entire thing is unfortunately tainted with my notorious sense of humour', he had written to him. It is his Pastoral Symphony, in which his affinity with nature is the prime element. 'I saw Pan within him,' Walter wrote; and indeed Mahler thought of calling the symphony *Pan*. 'It always strikes me as odd,' Mahler wrote to Richard Batka in November 1896, 'that most people when they speak of "nature", think only of flowers, little birds and the scent of the pine forest. No one knows the god Dionysus or the great Pan. There now! You have a sort of programme—that is, a sample of how I make music. Everywhere and always, it is only the voice of nature!' [6] The second movement, the minuet—'the fashionable flower piece'— was performed separately by Nikisch and Felix Weingartner in the winter of 1896. Mahler realized that, played out of context, this movement could give a false impression of the symphony

[6] A. Mahler (ed.), *Gustav Mahler's Letters 1879–1911* (Berlin, 1924), pp. 214–15.

but, he told Batka, 'if I want at long last to get a hearing I must not be too sensitive'.

This closeness to nature, which we today might call escapism, would hardly have been suspected by some who had worked with him in Hamburg. It was the same mood that made him speculate on the likely result of his going to Vienna:

What would result from my ways of handling affairs? I need only try to teach the famous Philharmonic, trained by honest Hans [Richter], what my ideas of a Beethoven symphony are, to become immediately involved in the ugliest struggle. . . . My only wish is to work in a little town, where there are no 'traditions' and no guardians of 'the eternal laws of beauty', among simple people, and to satisfy within the smallest circle myself and the few who are willing to follow me.

Music was not merely a profession for Mahler; it was a sacred mission, to which everyone and everything took second place. He explained his absorption in composition in a letter to his mistress Anna von Mildenburg dated 29th June 1896: 'One is nothing but an instrument on which the universe plays. . . . All those who live with me have had to learn this. At such times I don't belong to myself. I cannot be otherwise . . . . The creator . . . must endure many hours of solitude and of absence during which he is lost in himself and entirely cut off from the outside world.' Those are almost exactly the words of his most famous song written five years later: 'Ich bin der Welt abhanden gekommen' ('I am lost to the world').

5 Vienna

When Mahler left Vienna in 1907 he described his decade at the Opera as 'ten war-years'. Arnold Schoenberg, in a letter to him in 1910, referred to 'our hated and beloved Vienna'. From his days at the Conservatory Mahler knew only too well how Vienna treated its great men, canonizing them when they were dead, often reviling them during their lifetime. The city repelled him yet fatally attracted him. It was, after all, the city of Haydn, Mozart, Beethoven, Schubert and Bruckner, the city of the Strauss waltz, of the coffee-houses, of the Prater and the Opern-ring. The city of light-hearted, easy-going, gracious living, of intrigue, callousness and spite where revolutionary ideas in art struggled for expression in a climate of conservative, sometimes reactionary, opinion. The years from 1897 to 1914 were Vienna's 'Edwardian' age, an almost exact parallel to the London of the same period. With hindsight, it seems that the life of Europe then was illuminated by a garish light shed by the sun as it gradually became obscured by the storm clouds. In Vienna the opera had a golden age under Mahler; the operettas of Lehár and Oscar Straus were on everyone's lips; science and medicine thrived; writers and painters abounded. But the Emperor was growing old; the political scene was seething; anti-Semitism grew fiercer and more open.

Mahler, as artistic director of the Royal and Imperial Opera, was responsible only to the Emperor's Lord Chamberlain of the Household, Prince Montenuovo, who supported him through many crises. From the day he took up his post Mahler set musical

Vienna by the ears. 'As a man I am willing to make every possible concession,' he said, 'but as a musician I make none. Other opera directors look after themselves and wear out the theatre. I wear myself out and look after the theatre.' Gossip columnists seized on every scrap of information about him, true or false. Anything he said at rehearsals was 'news'. Public and performers alike were disciplined. He re-introduced Wagner's custom of dimming the house lights before the curtain rose. Latecomers were shut out until Act I was over. More and stricter rehearsals were held and no excuses for absence were accepted, however luminous the star concerned. The orchestral players' custom of sending deputies was outlawed. Wagner's operas were given complete. He eliminated spurious top notes and cadenzas inserted into Mozart by some singers.

Mahler supervised every detail of the operas (the very idea of an independent producer would have horrified him). Lighting, costumes, décor, acting—all these he rigorously controlled, in pursuit of his ideal of opera as an art form in which music, drama, ballet and design played equal parts. But his first task in his early years was to impose his musical standards on the singers. He found he could not work with some of the 'old guard'; they found him tyrannical, overbearing and rude. So they left, and he built up a new company of his own choice, among them Anna von Mildenburg, Marie Gutheil-Schoder, Selma Kurz, Erik Schmedes, Leo Slezak, Leopold Demuth, Friedrich Weidemann and Richard Mayr. (And in those days, of course, they stayed in Vienna—they did not gad about the world in jet aircraft.) He constantly gave young singers chances in major rôles; as frequently he dropped them if he realized he had misjudged their potentiality.

He was criticized because he sometimes preferred less-than-perfect singers with outstanding acting ability to those who had only 'a lovely voice' (a parallel with Verdi, who advised impresarios to engage Victor Maurel for Iago even if he could only speak the part, because he acted it so superbly). He pointed

out to a friend that Mildenburg had not always been 'the greatest
dramatic actress of our day' until

> I taught her to watch every one of her actions, every gesture and
> expression, in the mirror as part of her musical drill. . . . When she had
> learned her part, I taught her every step, every position, every move-
> ment. . . . At first sight Schoder seems insignificant as a woman, her
> voice is mediocre and not even that in the middle register. Yet every
> note of hers is full of feeling and each expression embodies the
> personality of the character she is playing.

His *tempi* in Wagner, so different from Richter's, aroused
controversy. Told that such things were traditional, he replied:
'What you theatre folk call your tradition is really nothing but
your comfort and your laziness.' His refusal to join any cliques,
inability to dissemble, to conceal his contempt for the second-
rate, or to learn tact, made him enemies even among those who
approved of what he was trying to achieve. There were no half-
measures on either side. Cheers and boos mingled to greet his
arrival at the desk. His enlightened policy of staging new works,
while acclaimed by the minority of progressives, enraged and
estranged the multitude. Some of the older singers, of course,
acknowledged his worth. Theodor Reichmann, a great Sachs and
Wotan, who privately called Mahler 'the Jewish monkey'
because of the way he would leap from the rostrum and scramble
through the double basses on to the stage at rehearsals, nevertheless wrote in his diary: 'The inspiration that radiates from the
little man is fantastic. He makes you give more than you ever
had.' Within a year the Emperor had personally congratulated
Mahler on 'making himself the master of conditions at the
Opera'. Mahler even scored over the royal household. Told that
one of the royal family wanted the Hofoper to perform an opera
by his Budapest adversary Count Zichy, Mahler said to Montenuovo: 'Very well, but I will state in the programme that it is
staged "by imperial command".' This was reported to Franz

Joseph, who said: 'I will certainly not *command* such a thing.'
Mahler was incorruptible, and he even tried to abolish the *claque*,
though the singers defeated him.

His relationship with Richter, as could be expected, was
cool.[1] It is always said that Mahler drove him out; while this
may be partially true, because Mahler took over the Wagner
operas, it should be remembered that Richter had been formally
offered the conductorship of the Hallé Orchestra of Manchester
in November 1895, two years before Mahler took up his Vienna
post. He procrastinated for nearly four years on the grounds
that he was re-negotiating his Vienna pension. But from the first
he said he wanted to go to the Hallé, so we need not shed too
many tears for him. As his assistant conductors Mahler engaged
Franz Schalk, from 1900, and Bruno Walter, from 1901. Among
the contemporary operas produced during Mahler's tenure (not
all of them conducted by him) were Puccini's *Madama Butterfly*
and *La Bohème* (with Caruso as Rodolfo); Leoncavallo's *La
Bohème* and *Pagliacci*; Mascagni's *Cavalleria Rusticana*; Richard
Strauss's *Feuersnot*; Siegfried Wagner's *Bärenhäuter*; Reznicek's
Donna Diana; Charpentier's *Louise* and Hans Pfitzner's *Die Rose
vom Liebesgarten*. But it was in the revivals (in many cases this
was the *mot juste*) of the great classics that his most significant
work was done, in three works in particular: *Don Giovanni*,
Fidelio and *Tristan und Isolde*.

Bruno Walter and Erwin Stein have fortunately left us vivid
recollections of Mahler's greatest achievements. Stein describes [2]
his *Tristan* as 'feverish and even delirious'. It was in three

[1] Richter said to Busoni in London in June 1899: 'I have heard that Mahler
gave you a lesson in the rehearsal [for a Vienna Philharmonic concert]. That
is the limit! He doesn't like soloists because he has no routine and cannot
conduct at sight' (*Letters to His Wife*, F. Busoni. London, 1938, p. 31).

[2] The ensuing quotations are from E. Stein, *Mahler and the Vienna Opera*
in *The Opera Bedside Book*, ed. H. Rosenthal (London, 1965), pp. 296–
317, and from Walter's *Gustav Mahler*, op. cit.

central moods: 'unrelieved yearning, white-hot passion and violent suffering'. The climaxes were 'shattering indeed. To him they were not only a means of expression, but also a means of architecture'. Mildenburg's Isolde was a great tragic performance. The Tristan was Erik Schmedes. (It was to him that Mahler said: 'Well, my dear Schmedes, don't forget: before the love potion you are a baritone, after it a tenor', a remark of even more point when one knows that Schmedes had started his career as a baritone.) Under Mahler *Die Walküre* 'became a singers', almost a *bel canto*, opera. The huge *Ring* orchestra had to play with chamber-music delicacy. . . . He gave every phrase the utmost intensity of expression'.

The *Tristan* production, 21st February 1903 (to mark the twentieth anniversary of Wagner's death), was the beginning of Mahler's collaboration with the stage-designer Alfred Roller (1864–1935), a man as dedicated, uncompromising and pioneering as Mahler himself. He was a friend of Gustav Klimt, leader of the *Sezession* group of artists. Roller and Mahler discovered that they shared ideas on how to revitalize opera production. In *Tristan* Roller made use of kaleidoscopic light and colour effects and bathed Act II in violet to symbolize night. Mahler, before he met Roller, had replaced the pantomime spookery of the Wolf's Glen scene in *Der Freischütz* by an impressionistic display of light and shade and clouds.[3] Five Mozart operas were re-staged in 1906 to mark the 150th anniversary of the composer's birth. In *Don Giovanni* the famous 'Roller towers' were first used. These were two massive grey structures on either side of the stage and served as the Commendatore's house, Elvira's balcony, the Don's house, and tombstones, thus revolutionizing quick scene-changing. In Beethoven's *Fidelio* (1904) the first scene was restored to Rocco's lodge as in the 1806 version. The prisoners realistically came groping from a dark hole, with the guards

[3] See Prawy's *The Vienna Opera* (London, 1969) for a detailed account of these productions.

lurking in the shadows: the darkness of Roller's sets was a regular target for critics.

The 1906 revivals of *Die Entführung aus dem Serail* and of *Così fan tutte* were box-office failures (as was Verdi's *Falstaff* in 1904). In *Don Giovanni* and *Figaro* Mahler restored the *secco* recitatives, which he accompanied himself. He ended the former after the Don's descent into Hell, omitting the final sextet. 'Mahler', said Stein, 'was the ideal Mozart performer. He was capable of the exceedingly subtle rubato that is implied in Mozart's melodies. . . . There was always time for the music to sound and for the singer to sing.' In *Figaro* 'it was the leisure of even the quickest *tempi* that brought the points of music and play across. . . . The last finale . . . was built up as a great Nocturne, beginning in an atmosphere of curious suspense'. In order to make Marcellina's lawsuit clearer, he inserted the trial scene from Beaumarchais in *secco* recitative 'composed' for the production from Mozartian works.

The Mahler-Roller *Fidelio* (first produced 7th October 1904) was one of their finest achievements, distinguished by Mildenburg's legendary Leonora. Mahler 'did not try to smooth . . . Beethoven's occasional oddities and abruptnesses, but made the music sound as strange as it is conceived'. He considered the 1907 *Iphigénie en Aulide*, in Wagner's version of Gluck, 'the best that Roller and I have achieved so far'. Earlier triumphs included Tchaikovsky's *Pique-Dame*, of which he was very fond, Weber's *Euryanthe*, Goetz's *The Taming of the Shrew*, and Offenbach's *Tales of Hoffmann*. And on New Year's Eve he would conduct *Die Fledermaus* in aid of the staff's pension fund, with some of the stars of the casts of other operas singing in the chorus and champagne in the glasses.

Bruno Walter marvellously summed up Mahler's genius as a conductor of opera:

He lived in everything and everything lived in him. And no matter how foreign a sentiment might be to him, how contrary to his character, his imagination would enable him to place himself inside the most opposite person and in the strangest of situations. Thus, Mahler's heart was on the stage when he sat at the desk. He conducted or, rather, he produced the music in accordance with the drama.

Walter has also left us an account of the physical aspects of Mahler's conducting:

Boehler's excellent silhouette caricatures show the violent and drastic nature of his gestures during his first years in Vienna. . . . His agility at that time and also previously, in Hamburg, was astonishing. . . . As time went on, his attitude and gestures became quieter. . . . In his last years his conducting presented a picture of almost uncanny quiet, although the intensity of expression did not suffer by it.

This is corroborated by Richard Aldrich of the *New York Times*, reviewing a Mahler concert on 30th November 1908: 'He has absolutely none of the poses or ornate and unnecessary gestures of the "prima donna" conductor as he stands upon the platform, short in stature, without distinction of figure or manner, with the left hand occasionally thrust into his pocket.'

On Richter's resignation, the Vienna Philharmonic, a self-governing body, elected Mahler as his successor. (The same players constituted the opera orchestra.) From the start, in September 1898, there was tension between them. They resented his intolerance of slovenly performance and his habit of stamping his feet and pointing his baton at recalcitrant players. There was also an element of anti-Semitism. When a player remarked that Richter had been much tougher with them, his companion replied: 'Yes, but Richter's one of us. We can take it from him.' Mahler's programmes were always interesting, including Bruckner symphonies and his own First and Second Symphonies. But the orchestra resented the violent criticisms provoked by his re-orchestration of several classic scores—Beethoven's Seventh and Ninth Symphonies, for example, his arrangement of Beethoven's Op. 95 string quartet for full strings, and his extensive amend-

ments to the Schumann symphonies, all directed towards clarity
of sound, Mahler's ideal.[4] Relations worsened after Mahler took
the orchestra to give five concerts in Paris in June 1900, at the
time of the World Exhibition. These were unsuccessful with
some of the press and public, one of them coinciding with a
fearful migraine which nearly prostrated Mahler.[5]

On 24th February 1901 Mahler conducted a Philharmonic
concert in the afternoon and *Die Zauberflöte* at the Opera in
the evening. Afterwards he collapsed with a near-fatal haemor-
rhage from haemorrhoids which necessitated an immediate
operation, his third for this ailment. While he was convalescing at
Abbazia on the Adriatic the Philharmonic gave two concerts,
one conducted by the mediocre Joseph Hellmesberger, son of
the former director of the Conservatory, the other by Franz
Schalk. The critics were pointedly extravagant in their praise. On
his return, Mahler withdrew his candidacy for re-election to the
conductorship.

At one of his concerts with the Philharmonic, in February
1899, Mahler had conducted the first complete performance of
Bruckner's Sixth Symphony—two movements only had been
performed sixteen years earlier—even though the work was
heavily cut. At this point it is worth glancing at Mahler's attitude
to the music of some of his great contemporaries, bearing in
mind that he was a creature of impulse, prone to swift and
sudden changes of mind. Discussing Bruckner with his brother
Otto in 1893, Mahler (according to Natalie Bauer-Lechner, who
noted the conversation [6]) spoke of being 'carried away by the
greatness and wealth of Bruckner's invention, but every now
and again you are disturbed . . . by its piecemeal character.' He
acknowledged Brahms as the greater, viewing their work as a

[4] See Appendix E.

[5] His programmes included Berlioz's *Symphonie Fantastique* and the
Scherzo of Bruckner's Fourth Symphony.

[6] N. Bauer-Lechner, *Memories of Gustav Mahler* (Leipzig, 1923), p. 16.

whole. Yet, eleven years later, writing to Alma he described Brahms and Bruckner as 'an odd pair of second-raters', Brahms being (musically) 'a puny little dwarf with a rather narrow chest. . . . It is very seldom he can make anything of his themes, beautiful as they often are'. Yet his deeds were better than his words in Bruckner's case, and he kept faith with the promise he made in a letter to the composer in 1886 'to help your glorious art to the triumph it deserves'. He conducted the *Te Deum* twice in Hamburg (1892 and 1893), the Mass in D Minor (1893) and the Third Symphony (1895). With the Vienna Philharmonic he also conducted the Fourth and Fifth Symphonies, but cut them.

For Richard Strauss, four years his junior, whom he had first met in Leipzig in 1887, he had mingled admiration and contempt, finding that the music too often reflected defects of personal character. The constant talk of royalties and percentages bored Mahler. 'Strauss sheds such a blight,' he wrote to Alma in February 1902. 'Better by far to eat the bread of poverty and follow one's star than sell one's soul like that. . . . My day will be when his has ended.' Alma, as is evident from her book, detested Strauss; one should therefore remember Mahler's remarks to Arthur Seidl written in February 1897:

I shall never forget how much I owe to Strauss . . . for he very unselfishly helped me to get a start. To consider me his rival, as many do already, is not at all something I should like to encourage. . . . I consider it my greatest joy to have found in one of my contemporaries such a fellow fighter and co-worker as Strauss. . . . When you call Strauss and me the 'opposite' poles of the modern magnetic axis, you say aloud an opinion I have harboured secretly for a long time.

In 1907 in Berlin Mahler attended two performances of *Salome*, in which Destinn sang. 'It is emphatically a work of genius . . . one of the greatest masterpieces of our time,' was his verdict. The censor had forbidden Mahler's proposed Vienna production in 1905; Mahler offered his resignation but it was refused. He was bored by *Elektra* in New York in 1910. Of Puccini Mahler held a poor opinion—'nowadays any bungler orchestrates to perfection', he said of *Tosca*—nor did he think much of Reger and Pfitzner. His famous remark about Hugo Wolf's songs was made to Oskar Fried in 1910: 'Of Wolf's one thousand songs I know only 344. Those 344 I do not like.' His 'gods' were Beethoven and Wagner, 'and after them, nobody'.

After the enormous effort involved in composing the Second and Third Symphonies and in putting the Opera on its feet, Mahler lay fallow during 1897 and 1898. He prepared the Second Symphony and *Lieder eines fahrenden Gesellen* for publication in 1897 and the often-revised First Symphony was published in 1899. In 1899 also he worked on a minor revision of his early cantata *Das klagende Lied* preparatory to publication in 1902. In 1899 he bought a plot of land at Maiernigg on the Wörthersee in Carinthia and began to build a chalet. That summer he spent at Alt-Aussee, Styria, where in August he began what was to be his happiest, least spectre-ridden symphony, the Fourth. He completed it on 5th August of the following summer, 1900. On 17th February 1901 Mahler conducted *Das klagende Lied*—'the first work in which I found myself as "Mahler"'—in Vienna. That summer at Maiernigg he began work on the Fifth Symphony, and on settings of poems by Friedrich Rückert. But the most significant event of 1901 for him was a dinner party on 7th November, at the Vienna home of the Zuckerkandls, when he met the beautiful 22-year-old Alma Maria Schindler.[7] Eighteen days later, in Munich, he conducted the first performance of the Fourth Symphony.

Alma—a Roman Catholic who described herself at this time as 'sceptical'—was the daughter of the landscape painter Emil J. Schindler, who died in 1892. Five years later her mother married Carl Moll, one of the founders of the *Sezession* group of young

[7] Born 31st August 1879.

artists and architects. Alma was a musician and became the pupil of Alexander von Zemlinsky. A fellow pupil was Arnold Schoenberg. To Alma in 1901 Mahler, besides being nineteen years her senior, was known as the all-powerful conductor who was the prey of every young woman with operatic ambitions,[8] and as a composer whose First Symphony she had disliked and rejected. Her first impression was of a man who talked as if he was addressing a meeting. 'He had wielded power so long, encountering only abject submission on every hand, that his isolation had become loneliness.' Within five months they were married.

[8] When Mildenburg joined the Vienna company, Mahler ended his amorous relationship with her, for he knew how vulnerable his position was and how the Viennese would seize upon any hint of scandal. In 1900 he had a brief love affair with Selma Kurz, but he recognized his susceptibility to beautiful sopranos and trod warily.

6 Alma

Alma Mahler wrote two remarkable books: *Gustav Mahler* and her autobiography *And the Bridge is Love*.[1] After Mahler's death she became the mistress of Oskar Kokoschka, the painter, and married the architect Walter Gropius, founder of the Bauhaus, in 1915. Soon they parted and were divorced. By Gropius she had a daughter, Manon, whose death from polio at the age of eighteen is commemorated in Berg's Violin Concerto, with its dedication 'to the memory of an angel'. In 1929 she married the writer Franz Werfel and eventually settled in the United States, where she died in 1964. Although she lived to the hilt for fifty-three years after his death, one senses from her writing that Gustav Mahler, even when she reacted against his music, dominated her existence. Their marriage was, on the face of it, doomed to failure, yet despite storms and stresses it held because of Mahler's intense love for her. They were Hans Sachs and Eva personified. Her books are often fearfully inaccurate, they may have offended individuals, but by their frankness and tactlessness as an unlikeable self-portrait they give an unrivalled, if distorted, picture not only of Mahler but of a whole artistic circle. The letters Mahler wrote to her for ten years are a moving and vivid revelation of his real personality, belying the superficial impression of him as a neurotic megalomaniac teetering on the brink of madness, a misrepresentation for which Alma is largely responsible. She lays candid stress on his egocentricity, his

[1] Hutchinson (London, 1959).

43

intolerance, his incredible *gaucherie* in some personal dealings, but through her pages and through his letters shines a man with a keen sense of observation, a philosophical acceptance of human frailties, a sardonic sense of humour, an astute business mind and a touching capacity for real affection. He could laugh at himself: writing to Alma in 1910 he admitted he had lost his temper at a rehearsal of the Eighth Symphony but later: 'I came out of my corner like a sulky boy.' It is also clear that, despite her pretensions, he was by miles her intellectual superior. He was not 'self-centred' in the narrow meaning: he was centred on his religion, which was music. No doubt Alma resented this omnipotent rival, more seductive than any mistress.

The world can never repay her for her influence on Mahler's compositions. From 1880 to 1901 he had written four symphonies, a cantata and songs: no mean output for a busy conductor. Yet between 1902 and 1907 while in charge of the Vienna Opera and in increasing demand as a conductor of his own and others' symphonic work, he wrote four enormous symphonies and the *Kindertotenlieder*. In the last three years of his life he wrote three symphonies. A month after their meeting he wrote to her from Berlin, where he conducted the Fourth Symphony on 16th December: 'I should like now to have success, recognition, and all those other really quite meaningless things people talk of. I want to do you honour.' Their rapid engagement, as can easily be imagined, was the talk of Vienna. It can also easily be imagined in what a vulnerable position Alma found herself, the target for all who wished to try through her to influence the director of the Opera. He, too, was pathetically easy prey for 'friends' who took him every piece of café tittle-tattle about his fiancée. No wonder she intensely disliked some of those who had known him since before she was born.

It would be an intolerable slight on Mahler's memory if he were to be judged for evermore by the picture of him committed to paper by Alma. She represents him as so self-centred that he was incapable of real love for anyone else. His long and frequent letters to her when they were apart show that he was always deeply concerned about her health and happiness. It is he who has to complain time after time that he has not heard from her or received only a short note. Alma was a born seductress glorying, as such women do, in their powers. When she met Mahler she was passionately in love with Zemlinsky and ready to lose her virginity to him, even if it meant pregnancy. In her diary [2] she wrote of her doubts: 'Could I ever love Mahler as he deserves? ... I don't know my own heart.... Would Mahler encourage me to work? Would he stand by my art? Would he love me for it, as Alex does?' She chose Mahler because he was 'the purest, the greatest genius' she had met. She hoped he would 'raise her to his level'. Yet she admitted to herself that she was 'incapable of warmth of feeling. Everything about me is calculation, cold, cold calculation.' Mahler was under no illusion about the nature of her character: while they were engaged he reproved her for her constant flirting with other men and asked her to give up everything, including her composing, if she was to be his wife. She agreed.

Alma implies that Mahler was totally inexperienced with women until he met her. While his affairs were often platonic, others were not (Mildenburg in Hamburg, for instance), but he worried about marrying a beautiful and passionate woman nineteen years his junior. In the early days of 1902, however, they made love and Alma was pregnant when they were married on 9th March 1902. The next day Mahler's sister Justine married Arnold Rosé, the leader of the Vienna Philharmonic, with whom she had been having a clandestine affair for some time, a circumstance which in itself had a deleterious effect on the orchestra's relationship with their conductor. The Mahlers spent their honeymoon in Russia, where Mahler conducted three concerts in

[2] Quoted by Henri-Louis de la Grange in 'Mistakes about Mahler', *Music and Musicians*, October 1972, pp. 16–22.

St Petersburg. For the first time, Alma sat behind the orchestra to watch him: 'His exaltation when he was conducting was always intense and the sight of his face on these occasions, uplifted and open-mouthed, was so inexpressibly moving.'

Home in Vienna, at a flat in the Auenbruggergasse, Alma found that her husband was deeply in debt, largely because of Justine's improvident housekeeping. It took Alma five years to get matters under control. She accompanied him to Crefeld for the first performance of the Third Symphony on 9th June. (None of his symphonies had first performances in Vienna in his lifetime. He was scrupulous, as opera director, in refusing to promote his works there.) Alma shrewdly summed up the contemporary attitude to Mahler as 'the Great Director of the Opera who to please himself had composed a monstrous symphony'. But this performance was a triumph and was the beginning of a genuine enthusiasm for Mahler's works, at any rate outside Vienna. Elated, Mahler and Alma went to Maiernigg for their first summer together. He in his oldest clothes, they went for long walks. They rowed, swam and sunbathed. He was anxious to complete the Fifth Symphony, so he worked in his hut in a wood, and she sat in the house making a fair copy of his score. 'His life during the summer months,' she wrote, 'was stripped of all dross, almost inhuman in its purity.' By autumn the symphony was completed in short score; he orchestrated it fully during the winter, working before breakfast.

Their first child, a daughter, was born on 3rd November 1902; although known always by the affectionate pet name 'Putzi', she was christened Maria, after Mahler's mother. According to Freud, Mahler had wanted Alma to use her second name, Maria,[3] and to

[3] Again I feel the need for a pinch of salt. Mahler never used 'Maria' in his letters; in fact he seemed to derive pleasure from concocting numerous affectionate diminutives of Alma. And to name one's daughter after one's mother (and then call her by a nickname anyway) is surely a pretty compliment rather than an indication of an obsession.

46

look 'more stricken', reflecting justifiable distrust of her youth
and beauty and of the attentions paid to her by Hans Pfitzner and
other young men in her artistic circle. He tyrannized her in the
sense that he insisted on their life's subservience to music.
Nothing must disturb that. It was a severe burden to lay on a
young woman but, to her credit, she saw the cause of it—in
retrospect, at any rate: 'Work, exaltation, self-denial and the
never-ending quest were his whole life on and on and for ever.
. . . He noticed nothing of all it cost me. He was utterly self-
centred by nature, and yet he never thought of himself. His work
was all in all.'

And his work, quite apart from the Opera, increased during
1903. A happy experience awaited him in October when he first
conducted the Concertgebouw Orchestra of Amsterdam, whose
conductor Willem Mengelberg was a devout Mahlerian. He fell
in love with the orchestra ('glorious') and they with him; and
with the Dutch countryside: 'Enchanting roads, paved, and
lined with trees . . . and the long undeviating canals, converging
from every quarter, shining like streaks of silver, and the little
green-washed houses; and, above it all, the grey-blue, cloudy
sky and flocks of birds. So lovely.' After the Third Symphony
'the tumult of applause was almost daunting. Everyone said
nothing like it could be remembered. I have beaten Strauss, who
is all the rage here, by yards'.

That 1903 summer in Maiernigg saw the completion of two
movements of the Sixth Symphony and the composition of a
love-song for Alma, *Liebst du um Schönheit*: 'If you love for
love's sake, yes, then love me.' Their love that September led to
the birth of a second daughter, Anna, nicknamed Guckerl, in
Vienna on 15th June 1904. Earlier that year there had been more
performances of his symphonies, notably the Third, throughout
Germany. 'In your new toilette you're well up to my Third, well
performed,' he wrote to Alma. From him that was a compliment.
When they went with Putzi and the baby to Maiernigg, he com-

pleted the Sixth Symphony, made some sketches for the Seventh, and added two settings to three composed in 1901 of Rückert's poems mourning the death of children, *Kindertotenlieder*. Alma was horrified by the idea of these songs. 'For heaven's sake, don't tempt Providence,' she told him. He played her the completed symphony. 'We both wept that day'—so deeply were they affected by the personal nature of the music and especially by the three 'hammer-blows' in the finale. '"It is the hero, on whom fall three blows of fate, the last of which fells him as a tree is felled." Those were his words.' Although the load of debt and the anguish of sexual jealousies were eroding their marriage at this time, Mahler was at his peak. 'I don't know anybody who can do more than I can,' he boasted. He went straight from this holiday to launch his wonderful *Fidelio* production.

During 1904 the Philharmonic played through the Fifth Symphony with Mahler. Alma, who had copied it and knew it by heart, was mortified to hear that he had overscored the percussion so strongly that the themes were obscured. He agreed with her and made some revisions, the first of many. Because of illness she could not go with him to Cologne for the first performance on 18th October. He saw at his first rehearsal what difficulties he had created:

The Scherzo is the very devil of a movement. I see it is in for a peck of troubles! Conductors for the next fifty years will all take it too fast and make nonsense of it; and the public—oh, heavens, what are they to make of this chaos of which new worlds are for ever being engendered? . . . What are they to say to this primeval music, this foaming, roaring, raging sea of sound? . . . Oh that I had been born a commercial traveller and engaged as baritone at the Opera! [4] Oh that I might give my symphony its first performance fifty years after my death!

[4] A reference to Leopold Demuth.

And after the performance: 'The Fifth is an accursed work. No one understands it.'

He received pleasure from the friendliness shown to him by many of the orchestras he conducted, in contrast to the tensions of Vienna. At Leipzig, for instance: 'Yesterday and today I pitched into them for four hours at a stretch, and instead of taking it in bad part they bade me an enthusiastic farewell at the end of it.' He was beginning to realize too that the younger generation admired him. After the first performance of the Fourth Symphony in 1901 a sixteen-year-old boy, Alban Berg, stormed his dressing-room and carried off his baton as a memento. And Alma's friend Schoenberg, thirty years old in 1904, who had begun by disliking Mahler's music and had had many an argument with Mahler, wrote to him in December after hearing the Third Symphony in Vienna:

I saw your very soul naked, stark naked. . . . I felt your symphony. I shared in the battling for illusion; I suffered the pangs of disillusionment; I saw the forces of good and evil wrestling with each other; I saw a man in torment struggling towards inward harmony. . . . Forgive me, I cannot feel by halves.

If this language seems extravagant, it conveys the impact this music made when it was new. Mahler for his part was to demonstrate his belief in Schoenberg's music, even if he did not fully understand it. At the first performance of the Chamber Symphony No. 1, on 8th February 1907, he angrily silenced those who noisily pushed their chairs back during the performance; and at the end he stood applauding until everyone had left.

The year 1905 began for Mahler with the first performances, in Vienna, of *Kindertotenlieder* (29th January and 3rd February). During the year he conducted several performances of the Fifth Symphony and, at Maiernigg, completed the full sketch of the Seventh Symphony. He had composed the two *Andante* movements (Nos. 2 and 4) the previous summer, and in a letter written in May 1910 he gave Alma a vivid description of how the rest of the work was written in 1905:

In art as in life I am at the mercy of spontaneity. If I had to compose, not a note would come. . . . I made up my mind to finish the Seventh, both Andantes of which were then on my table. I plagued myself for two weeks until I sank into gloom. . . . then I tore off to the Dolomites. There I was led the same dance, and at last gave it up and returned home. . . . I got into the boat to be rowed across. At the first stroke of the oars the theme (or rather the rhythm and character) of the introduction to the first movement came into my head—and in four weeks, the first, third and fifth movements were done.

In those weeks when inspiration would not come, Mahler displayed his immense physical strength and energy—climbing, rowing, walking in the rain for five hours singing aloud as he composed—an alarming sight to come upon unawares, as a child named Rudolf Bing did.[5] To Alma, who had been urged by a Dr Roșthorn to ask him to rest, he contemptuously replied: 'Your Rosthorns have not the dimmest notion of an entelechy such as mine. . . . They cannot imagine the evil effects on me of not sticking to my work.' Alma has depicted Mahler as a weakly hypochondriac. Yet he was very tough and, apart from migraines and ominously recurrent sore throats, was hardly ever ill; in fact he regarded illness with scorn. He was a frugal eater and moderate drinker: he trained like an athlete for his work.

In March 1906 he was again in Amsterdam for performances of the Fifth Symphony, *Das klagende Lied* and *Kindertotenlieder*. 'Mengelberg is a man you can rely on,' he told Alma. 'I have true friends here.' On his return he played through the Sixth Symphony with the Vienna Philharmonic, but the first performance was to be at a festival at Essen on 27th May. Mahler had a week of rehearsals, which went well and were brightened further by his first meeting with the Russian pianist

[5] Sir Rudolf Bing, *5000 Nights at the Opera* (London, 1972), p. 8.

and conductor, Ossip Gabrilovitch, then aged twenty-eight. Alma joined him for the dress reheasal. 'You are in for a treat,' he told her. But at the last rehearsal the tragic intensity of the music—and, perhaps, its technical difficulty—overwhelmed him and afterwards he 'walked up and down in the artists' room, sobbing, wringing his hands, unable to control himself' while Alma and some of his friends looked on, aghast. Into this scene irrupted Richard Strauss, bringing a trivial piece of news and exclaiming insensitively: 'What's up with you?' [*] Mahler was so worried that his feelings might again master him at the first performance that, according to Alma, he did not conduct well. To Richard Specht he wrote: 'My Sixth will propound riddles the solution of which may be attempted only by a generation which has absorbed and truly digested my first five symphonies.' That forecast has been fulfilled. He was greatly affected by his own music. For instance, he wrote to Alma after conducting the First Symphony: 'Sometimes it sent shivers down my spine. Damn it all, where do people keep their ears and their hearts if they can't hear *that*!'

At Maiernigg that summer, on the first day of the holiday, he 'went up to the hut with the firm resolution of idling the holiday away (I needed to so much that year) and recruiting my strength. On the threshold of my old workshop the *Spiritus Creator* took hold of me and shook me and drove me on for the next eight weeks until my greatest work was done.' So we know that the gigantic Eighth Symphony was written in an astonishingly brief period. Its first part is a setting of the hymn *Veni Creator Spiritus*, its second a setting of the last scene of *Faust*. He interrupted its composition to conduct *Figaro* at the Salzburg Festival where the critic Julius Korngold noticed that 'a much-

---

[*] Strauss, it should be remembered, was as great and as professional a conductor as Mahler. He was sympathizing over a last-minute alteration to the programme and, with his detached attitude to his own music, he would never have envisaged Mahler's emotional state.

thumbed volume [of *Faust*] protruded from his coat pocket'. He completed the sketch on 18th August and elatedly wrote that day to Mengelberg: 'It is the biggest thing I have done so far. . . . Imagine that the universe begins to vibrate and to sound. These are no longer human voices but planets and sun rotating.'

The climactic year of 1907 [7] began for Mahler with a gloom which was to increase. From Frankfurt in January he wrote to Alma: 'I am a hunted stag, hounds in full cry. . . . What is the good of being pelted with mud time after time. The curs obviously take me for a lamp-post.' This outburst followed a savaging of his Third Symphony by the Berlin critics. 'I cannot even orchestrate, it seems.' But other clouds were gathering. 'All the newspapers [in Frankfurt] have reports from Vienna of my resignation. Does it mean there is another outcry because of my prolonged absence? The newspapers . . . say that I have piled up an enormous deficit, that I have become impossible, etc. etc.'

A crisis at the Opera had been brewing for some time. It was true that expenditure had risen—largely because of Roller's designs—and box-office takings had fallen. Mahler's enemies were ever ready to strike, to attack him direct or through his protégé, Bruno Walter. Increasing anti-Semitism was the background to this intensified campaign. Prince Montenuovo had hitherto supported Mahler, but even between them relations began to cool. Mahler, out of loyalty, had taken Roller's side in a dispute between Montenuovo and Roller when Roller was flagrantly in the wrong. This gave the Chamberlain an opening for further protests about Mahler's absences to conduct elsewhere. The Prince had some cause to complain. Ida Dehmel, in her diary for March 1905, records Mahler as saying: 'I should like best to live only for my compositions and, to tell the truth, I am beginning to neglect my operatic duties.' He explained that bad

[7] Alma Mahler's account of the last four years of their lives together has several inaccuracies and inconsistencies and its chronology is suspect.

Gustav Mahler in Hamburg in 1896

Left A silhouette drawn in Vienna, 1901
Right Cartoon of Mahler the conductor

Mahler relaxing on board ship

Gustav and Alma with Maria and Anna (foreground) at Maiernigg in
1906

Mahler and his wife, Alma, in Rome in 1910

A page from the manuscript of *Das Lied von der Erde*

Rodin's bust of Mahler, 1909

Mahler in 1907 in the Vienna Opera House

performances of his Fifth Symphony under other conductors had reinforced his view that 'a musical score is a book with seven seals. . . . There must be a tradition and no one can create it but I'.

In this frame of mind, on 31st March 1907, he handed Montenuovo his resignation. Although he knew he could have won yet another battle, he had had enough. Talking to Bruno Walter, he shook the legs of a chair and said: 'You see, that's what they are now doing to me: if I were to want to remain seated, all I would have to do is to lean back firmly and I could hold my own. But I am not offering any resistance, and so I shall finally slide down.' In a conversation with Natalie Bauer-Lechner in 1906 he had spoken of his determination to resign in 1907 because he was tired of repertory opera. He added:

All things have their day and I have had mine and so has my work as the local opera director. I am no longer 'news' as far as Vienna is concerned. So I want to go at a point when I can still expect that, at a later date, the Viennese will learn to appreciate what I did for their theatre.

Efforts to find a successor were not immediately fruitful, and Montenuovo tried to persuade Mahler to change his mind. But on 10th August he wrote to say that Weingartner would take up the post on 1st January 1908 and that the Emperor had granted Mahler a pension more than double that to which he was entitled, a large compensatory payment and a promise that Alma, after his death, would be 'entitled to the pension of the widow of a Privy Councillor (although you did not rank as such)'. He was handsomely treated. Montenuovo's letter ended: 'Conried need now delay no longer making your engagement public.' This referred to Heinrich Conried, director of the Metropolitan Opera, New York, since 1903, who had approached Mahler earlier in the year with an offer of a four-year contract. Mahler wanted one for only one year. On 5th

Mahler

June in Berlin they clinched an engagement for the first four months of 1908 at a salary of $20,000.

Overshadowing these negotiations was Mahler's health. Most accounts of this year in Mahler's life seem to telescope events which were in fact considerably spread out, as the documents show. It would seem that he had first consulted their family doctor Blumenthal early in January 1907 before he went to conduct the Third Symphony in Berlin and the Fourth in Frankfurt. In a letter to Alma from Frankfurt on 17th January 1907 occur the lines: 'You see, Almschili, one does not die of it—look at Mama with her heart—one goes full speed ahead and then suddenly comes the crash.' Writing to her on 30th March, while she was convalescing from a throat operation he said:

I had myself inoculated yesterday by Dr Hamperl, who examined me too at the same time. He found a *slight* valvular defect, which is entirely compensated, and he makes nothing of the whole affair. He tells me I can certainly carry on with my work just as I did before and in general live a normal life, apart from avoiding over-fatigue. It is funny that in substance he said just what Blumenthal said, but his whole way of saying it was somehow reassuring. Also I find I have no fear of conducting now.

This heart lesion was the tell-tale sign of the inexorable progress of subacute bacterial endocarditis, the legacy of infection from his persistent 'bad throats'.

Determined on resignation from Vienna and with his visit to New York settled, Mahler took Alma and the children to Maiernigg towards the end of June. On the third day of the holiday their elder daughter Maria ('Putzi') developed scarlet fever and diphtheria. After a fortnight's struggle and an unsuccessful tracheotomy she died on 5th July, aged four and a half. Mahler was stricken. He had adored this beautiful child. 'Each morning', Alma wrote, 'Putzi would go into Mahler's study where they had long talks. Nobody has ever known what about. . . . By the time

54

Mahler brought her back she was usually smeared with jam from top to toe. . . . They were so happy together.' Alma collapsed from exhaustion and Blumenthal, after examining her, again checked Mahler's heart. He advised him to consult Professor Kovacs in Vienna. Kovacs, it appears, told him the condition was serious and that he must shepherd his strength if it was not to prove rapidly fatal. It is unlikely that he pronounced a death-sentence in so many words, but Mahler drew the inevitable conclusion. He and Alma spent the next few weeks at Schluder-bach in the Tyrol. To distract himself, Mahler read *Die chinesische Flöte* (*The Chinese Flute*), an anthology by Hans Bethge, based on ancient Chinese poems, which a friend had given to him on its publication by Leipzig Insel-Verlag earlier in the year with the suggestion that some of the poems might be made into songs. According to Alma, Mahler sketched some settings while at Schluderbach.

In the middle of August he returned to supervise his last productions at the Opera, where he was 'welcomed respectfully and cordially by all'. His final performance, *Fidelio*, was on 15th October. It was thinly attended. In early November he went to St Petersburg, revising his Fifth Symphony on the journey. Among those who heard and liked it there was the young Stravinsky. In Helsinki Mahler heard the music of Sibelius— 'hackneyed clichés'—and met the composer—'extremely sympathetic'. It was then that they had their famous discussion on the symphony. Back in Vienna he said farewell to his public at a special performance of his Second Symphony on 24th November by the Court Opera Orchestra and choral society. There was a 'hurricane of applause' which moved him to tears.

On 7th December he issued a farewell message to the Opera: 'I leave patchwork, the incomplete, as man is fated to do. . . . I meant well and aimed high. . . . I have always given my all. . . . In the crush of the struggle, in the heat of the moment, wounds were sustained, errors committed, by you as well as by me.' It

was pinned to the notice-board. Next day it was ripped down
and torn into pieces. This was symbolic of the manner in which
Mahler was treated by Vienna, and indeed by the other cities
in which he worked, where his single-minded dedication made
him enemies, especially among upholders of the 'traditions' he
renovated. (Yet Hanslick, to his credit, was one of his strongest
supporters in Vienna and had urged his appointment.) No
wonder Mahler referred to opera as 'shameless prostitution,
reducing noble material to dirt' when he met opposition to
all his reforms. The virulent and personally hostile press
criticism of Mahler throughout his career has to be read to be
believed. Much of it was directed against his racial origin. 'The
Jewish dwarf', someone called him, little knowing of Mahler's
sense of humour in that respect. For in 1898, criticizing a tenor
who had caricatured the Jewish traits of the dwarf, Mime, in
Siegfried, he had written self-revealingly to Natalie Bauer-
Lechner: 'I know of only one Mime, and that is me. . . . You
wouldn't believe what there is in that part nor what I could
make of it!'

Leaving their daughter Anna with Alma's mother, Mahler and
Alma left Vienna for Cherbourg on 9th December. Schoenberg,
Walter, Roller and Zemlinsky were among those who went to the
station to wish them *bon voyage*. The playwright Gerhart
Hauptmann telegraphed to Mahler: 'Europe . . . needs men like
you as it does its daily bread.'

7 New York

They arrived in New York the week before Christmas. Anna had been left with Alma's mother, so the loss of Putzi was even more poignantly felt by them both. But for Mahler there was the Metropolitan Opera.

His impact on the New York scene was awaited apprehensively. An article in the *New York Mail* of 23rd September 1907 speculated about happenings at the Metropolitan under one who 'is no respecter of anything but his art. The "stars" may be compelled to drop from their height and take rehearsals like ordinary mortals . . . and they may be compelled to accept comments not in harmony with their opinion of themselves.' This publication also printed a candid description of Mahler by a young American conductor, Walter Rothwell, who had seen him in Europe:

Where all others end he begins. . . . He has many peculiarities which cannot in any way be explained. As example, innumerable times I have seen men in his orchestra lay down their instruments absolutely like paralysed, unable to sound a note, the only cause being the look in his eyes. I have heard them say 'I cannot play a note until you take your eyes off me'. He can secure almost any effect he desires through those wonderful eyes. Not by reason of his personality, because I do not think that anyone would call it agreeable. . . . His most distinguishing feature is his wonderful power of becoming two men—a Mozart conductor and a Wagner conductor.

Mahler's first opera at the Metropolitan was *Tristan und Isolde* on 1st January 1908, with Olive Fremstad singing her first Isolde and Heinrich Knote as Tristan. 'The influence of the new conductor was felt and heard in the whole spirit of the performance,' Richard Aldrich wrote in the *New York Times*. 'Through it all went the pulse of dramatic beauty.'

Mahler was elated by the quality of the singers available; he seemed easier-going than in Vienna and made all the usual cuts in Wagner (perhaps to spare himself). The cast for his first *Don Giovanni* on 23rd January was Antonio Scotti (Don Giovanni), Feodor Chaliapin (Leporello), Alessandro Bonci (Don Ottavio), Emma Eames (Donna Anna), Johanna Gadski (Donna Elvira) and Marcella Sembrich (Zerlina). At a later performance Geraldine Farrar sang Zerlina. On 7th February he conducted *Die Walküre*, with Gadski as Brünnhilde, Alois Burgstaller as Siegmund, Anton van Rooy as Wotan, Louise Kirkby-Lunn as Fricka and Fremstad as Sieglinde. In *Siegfried*, 19th February, Fremstad sang Brünnhilde. *Fidelio* was given on 20th March with a replica of Roller's sets. (Mahler hoped to obtain for Roller a post in New York, but by this time had abandoned the idea.) Berta Morena sang Leonora and Carl Burrian was Florestan.

What Mahler did not know was that Conried's days as director were already numbered. Desperate to withstand competition from Oscar Hammerstein's Manhattan Opera House, which opened on 3rd November 1907, Conried had engaged Mahler as one of his 'last throws', but even at the time of their Berlin meeting Otto H. Kahn, one of the Metropolitan leading backers, was in Paris persuading Giulio Gatti-Casazza, director of the Scala, Milan, to go to New York on the assumption that ill health would soon compel Conried's resignation, as it did.[1] If Gatti went to New York it meant that he would take Arturo Toscanini with him; hence Mahler's presence was an embarrassment to the Metropolitan board. Opera politics were not Vienna's copyright. When Kahn made a formal offer to

[1] He died on 27th April 1909.

Gatti and Toscanini in 1908 he asked for assurances that Toscanini would accept the Mahler situation. 'I hold Mahler in great esteem', was the reply. But Mahler was suspicious of Toscanini, as he had every right to be, and his fears were confirmed when the Italian insisted that *Tristan* should be ceded to him. In a letter to Andreas Dippel, associate director of the Metropolitan, before the 1908–9 season, Mahler wrote:

It is inconceivable to me that a new production of *Tristan* should be put on without my being consulted in any way and I cannot give my consent. . . . If recently—out of consideration for the wishes of my colleague [Toscanini]—I gave a free hand to the new director, it was with the express exception of *Tristan*. I took very special pains with *Tristan* last season and can well maintain that the form in which this work now appears in New York is my spiritual property.

For one season his wishes prevailed. Yet Toscanini opened the season on 16th November 1908 with *Aïda* (Emmy Destinn as Aïda, Caruso as Radames). Mahler returned on 13th January 1909 with Mozart's *Marriage of Figaro*, after twenty rehearsals. The cast included Eames, Sembrich and Farrar, with Scotti as the Count and Adamo Didur (a bass) as Figaro. On 19th February he conducted Smetana's *The Bartered Bride*, with Destinn as Marie and dancers imported from Prague. Then on 12th March came *Tristan*, with Fremstad and Burrian. A critic wrote that 'Mr Mahler turned loose such a torrent of vital sound as he had never before let us hear'. It was after this performance that he said to Alma: 'The stars were kind. I have never known a performance of *Tristan* to equal this.' He never conducted it again; and he conducted only one more opera—Tchaikovsky's *Pique-Dame* on 5th March 1910, with Leo Slezak as Hermann and Destinn as Lisa, its first performance in the United States. Alma describes Mahler at this period as 'in the best of health' after the critical summer of 1908 (see next chapter). She even persuaded him to accompany her to some dinner parties (not his favourite recreation) in the homes of the eccentric rich who financed the city's music-making.

During his second visit Mahler conducted three concerts by Walter Damrosch's New York Symphony Society on 30th November, 8th December and 13th December 1908. For the second concert the Oratorio Society joined the orchestra for his Second Symphony, its first New York performance. A few days later he was approached by four women supporters of the sixty-six-year-old New York Philharmonic Society which had been in the doldrums for some time. The society's orchestra had lost many of its best players to the Metropolitan, which had formed two orchestras so that it could play in two cities on the same evening and thus out-trump Hammerstein's Manhattan Opera. The Philharmonic directors wanted an orchestra at least the equal of Boston's. To achieve this, and to combat the lure of the three opera orchestras, they realized they must offer the players permanent engagements under an outstanding conductor. This entailed abandoning the co-operative scheme, by which society members elected the conductor, and replacing it by a board of directors who managed the society and gave absolute artistic powers to the conductor. They raised a guarantee fund of over 80,000 dollars for three years and Mahler agreed to replace Wassily Safonoff and to train a new orchestra.

Elated by their capture of such a notable quarry on a three-year contract, the Philharmonic arranged two special concerts, on 31st March and 6th April 1909, to 'introduce' Mahler. He chose routine programmes,[2] but although the critics were impressed by the drive and élan of the playing, he himself was under no illusion about the task which faced him and the need for new players—especially among the woodwind, who failed abysmally in the *Siegfried Idyll*. (A few months later he con-

[2] 31st March: *Manfred*, Schumann; 7th Symphony, Beethoven; *Siegfried Idyll*, Wagner; Overture to *Tannhäuser*, Wagner; 6th April: Overture to *Egmont*, 9th Symphony, Beethoven.

ducted it with the Concertgebouw and wrote to Alma: 'Balm after the experience in New York'.) The performance of Beethoven's Ninth Symphony at the second concert evidently surprised all the critics by its impassioned grandeur and by the unaccustomed violence of the timpani in the scherzo. A writer in the *New York Press* for 5th April 1909 proved to be the shrewdest student of his city, however, when he wrote:

Evidently Mahler is not used to dealing with rough material. His interpretations, lucid, exquisitely balanced in dynamics, finely elaborated in every detail, require a well-nigh perfect instrument. . . . Let us hope that those persons who have the power of supporting a permanent orchestra and of engaging so priceless a conductor as Mahler will fully appreciate the value of a reorganised Philharmonic Society and the genius of the man in charge. Unfortunately, however, there are many wealthy and generous persons who can see no difference in the conducting of a Damrosch and a Mahler.

One ominous fact was that Mahler left a sick-bed against doctor's orders to conduct the first of these concerts. He was reported as having influenza, but it is clear that this was an attack of the fever associated with the streptococcal infection that was to kill him.

Mahler opened the Philharmonic's sixty-eighth season on 4th November 1909. The new orchestra had ninety-five players, under a new leader, Theodore Spiering. The woodwind were strengthened and there were fewer strings but in better proportion: eight double basses, for example, instead of fourteen. In addition to the regular Thursday evening and Friday afternoon concerts (with the same programme) the season was expanded to include Sunday concerts, a Beethoven cycle and an historical cycle, forty-six in all. A special series was arranged for Brooklyn, and Mahler took the orchestra on its first tour: to New Haven, Springfield, Providence, Philadelphia and Boston, with Berlioz's *Fantastic Symphony* as the showpiece.

It is worth looking in detail at the programmes of Mahler's two Philharmonic seasons. They were designed to train the orchestra and, although they included 'novelties', these were by no means of such an enterprising kind as had distinguished the Symphony Society's programmes for several years in spite of critical discouragement. Safonoff had tried to brighten the Philharmonic programmes by introducing new Russian composers such as Skriabin, but had been taken to task by the critics. In 1909–10 Mahler's novelties included Dukas's *L'Apprenti Sorcier*, Debussy's *Nocturnes*, Busoni's *Turandot* suite ('With what love and unerring instinct this man rehearsed!' Busoni wrote to his wife ³), Bruckner's Fourth Symphony ⁴ (30th March 1910), Pfitzner's *Christelflein* overture, Dvořák's *Scherzo Capriccioso*, Rakhmaninov's D minor concerto (with the composer as soloist, 16th January 1910), and an evening of Bach, Handel, Haydn, Rameau and Grétry. Among soloists were Kreisler in the Brahms and Beethoven concertos, Josef Lhevinne in Tchaikovsky's First Piano Concerto and Busoni in Beethoven's Fifth Piano Concerto. He conducted his own First Symphony on 16th and 17th December 1909, and *Kindertotenlieder* on 26th and 28th January (the latter at Brooklyn) with Ludwig Wüllner as soloist ('in singularly poor voice,' said the *New York Times* critic).

The 1910–11 season, when he conducted forty of a contracted fifty-five programmes, included Strauss's *Also sprach Zarathustra*

³ *Letters to His Wife*, op. cit., p. 161.

⁴ Alma Mahler's statement, repeated in other books, that Mahler conducted all Bruckner's symphonies in New York is nonsense. The Fourth was the sole performance. Bruckner did not lack champions in the United States. First performances of the symphonies in New York were: No. 3, 5th December 1885 (W. Damrosch); No. 4, 16th March 1888 (Seidl); No. 5, 14th December 1911 (Stransky); No. 7, 13th November 1886 (T. Thomas, after an earlier Chicago performance); No. 8, 6th December 1906 (Boston Symphony Orchestra, Karl Muck); No. 9, 7th November 1907 (Boston and Muck).

and *Ein Heldenleben*; the ballet music from Mozart's *Idòmeneo*; Debussy's *Rondes de printemps*; Schumann's Second Symphony; Elgar's *Enigma Variations* and *Sea Pictures* (excluding 'The Swimmer'; the soloist was Kirkby-Lunn); Tchaikovsky's Second Symphony; a French programme including Debussy's *Ibéria*, Bizet's *L'Arlésienne* Suite No. 1 (with chorus), Chabrier's *España* and works by Massenet and Lalo; three excerpts from Berlioz's *Roméo et Juliette*; Stanford's *Irish Symphony*; Mac-Dowell's D minor Piano Concerto; and many Wagner items. Of his own music there was only *Ging heut' Morgen* and *Rhein-legendchen* (22nd and 25th November 1910, sung by Alma Gluck)[5] and the Fourth Symphony (17th and 20th January 1911, soprano Bella Alten).[6] His last concert on 21st February 1911 was an Italian programme with works by Sinigaglia, Martucci, Bossi and Busoni. The remainder of the season, while he was ill, was conducted by Spiering, the leader. Among the works Mahler had scheduled but did not conduct was Sibelius's Violin Concerto. It is known too that he intended in his third season to include a symphony by Charles Ives.

Although Alma glosses over the facts, perhaps because she eventually made America her home, Mahler's short spell with the Philharmonic was a failure. After his death the *New York Tribune* wrote: 'He was looked upon as a great artist, and possibly he was one, but he failed to convince the people of New York of the fact and, therefore, his New York career was not a success.' Why not? As with the Vienna Philharmonic, he aroused the dislike of many of the players. There is no doubt

[5] The concerts this season were on Tuesdays and Fridays.
[6] Apart from the three symphonies Mahler himself conducted in New York, No. 4 had previously been given in New York by the Symphony Society (W. Damrosch) on 6th November 1904 and No. 5 by the Boston Symphony Orchestra (Wilhelm Gericke) on 15th February 1906. The first American performance of the Fifth was by the Cincinnati Orchestra (Frank van der Stucken) on 24th March 1905.

that he would pick on and persecute a weak instrumentalist. He
foolishly made friends with one particular player, T. E. Johner,
a second violinist, who told him all the tittle-tattle and exacer-
bated Mahler's dislike of some other members of the orchestra,
which he realized needed much severe training. Not all the
orchestra 'hated him', as Alma has said. Some of the survivors
from those days whose reminiscences can be heard on a fascinating recording [7] make it clear that those who shared his
ideals loved him too. His beat was hard to follow—a 'bad
beat', some say—but the expressiveness of his hands and eyes
conveyed his meaning. He aimed especially for flexibility and
constant subtle variations of *tempo*; he wanted a lot of *portamento*
and *vibrato* from the strings and constantly sang to the orchestra
to illustrate the phrasing he sought. Whatever the work, one
player said in a telling comparison, Toscanini always remained
Toscanini, but Mahler entered into the spirit of each composer.
The finest tribute to him at this period in his life was paid in a
letter from Busoni, who was soloist at several concerts with him:
'Being with you has a sort of purifying effect. One has only to
come near you to feel young again.'

Mahler soon discovered that he was a prisoner of that fearful
matriarchy which has blighted so much of New York's musical
life and blasted the hopes of other conductors since his day. The
ladies of the committee soon found—as the Viennese had—
that Mahler could not be bent to their will nor would he attend
social gatherings, and if he did he was liable to be outspoken.
He would not popularize the programmes as they wished. Alma,
herself said: 'He performed a great deal of music merely to hear
it himself and to get to know it, without bothering whether it
went down with the public.'

Alma said that he was not criticized in New York as he had
been in Vienna. This is untrue. His own music was attacked—

[7] 'Gustav Mahler remembered', CBS–SBRG 72624 ℗ 1967.

'painfully cacophonous din' was a phrase used about the First Symphony by H. E. Krehbiel in the *World*—and there was severe complaint about his 'tampering' with other composers' scores. To quote Krehbiel again: 'Mahler was willing wantonly to insult the people's intelligence and taste by such things as multiplying the voices in a Beethoven symphony (additional kettledrums in the *Pastoral*, for example), by cutting down the strings and doubling the flutes in Mozart's G minor.' [8] Mahler, like many conductors of that day and since, did not regard the letter of the score as sacrosanct. He added an E♭ clarinet to the *Eroica* finale, telling the orchestra that it was a Hungarian tune and it ought to sound like gipsy music; he added instruments to Strauss's *Don Juan*, explaining that 'Strauss was a young man when he wrote it; he would score it differently now'. He liked double woodwind in Beethoven and Brahms.

In the middle of February 1911 Mahler was summoned to a full committee meeting, accused of various transgressions and informed of a severe limitation of his powers. His informant in the orchestra was dismissed. On 20th February he had a recurrence of a throat ailment which had afflicted him before Christmas. The next day, although a fever had developed, he insisted on conducting, and despite utter exhaustion completed the whole concert (at which Toscanini was present). It was his last. After his return to Europe an American journalist interviewed Alma on 4th May. She told him that she attributed Mahler's illness 'to nervous prostration and its consequences caused by his unfortunate relations with the Philharmonic Society of New York. You cannot imagine what he suffered. . . . In New York, to his amazement, he had ten women ordering him about like a puppet'. This is at least indicative of the emotional atmosphere in New York, though a nonsensical medical diagnosis. Busoni, the first performance of whose *Berceuse élégiaque* Mahler had conducted

[8] *New York Times*, 19th May 1911.

at his last concert, wrote revealingly to his wife [9] on 30th March 1911:

Mahler has not conducted since 21st February. Spiering took his place on the 24th ... and will remain until the end of the season. It was very creditable that an averagely good violinist should show so much *présence d'esprit* and was able to carry through the performance fairly well. But——! The behaviour of the New York audience and the critics over the matter will remain in my memory as one of my most painful experiences. The sensation made by a leader of an orchestra being able to conduct unprepared has made a greater impression on them than Mahler's whole personality was ever able to do! Spiering has been exalted to the position of one of the greatest conductors, and they have spoken quite seriously about his continuing to fill the post. *Not one word of regret has fallen about Mahler's absence!!* One reads of such things happening in history, but when it is a personal experience, one is filled with despair.

When the Philharmonic gave a memorial concert for their late conductor on 23rd November 1911, they represented his genius as a composer by the first movement of the Fifth Symphony, nothing more. That too fills one with despair even now. His arrival in New York coincided with the beginning of its obsession with Toscanini. So the Metropolitan venture failed. He became involved with the Philharmonic, at a time of crisis and reorganization. Being the artist he was he strove for perfection, as he had in Vienna, but his method of striving created enemies all too easily, and New York, with its notoriously shallow and sensation-seeking approach to music, added him to its roll of sacrificial victims.

[9] *Letters to His Wife*, op. cit., p. 194.

8 'Abschied'

Mahler spent only parts of 1908–11 in New York. We must therefore go back to May 1908, when he returned to Europe to conduct his First Symphony at Wiesbaden. He had composed nothing in 1907 and there was no question of returning to Maiernigg with its painful memories. Alma found them a farmhouse outside the village of Toblach in the Dolomites, a region of unspoilt natural beauty. There in June he set to work again.

But now, perhaps for the first time, he fully realized the implications of his heart ailment. He wrote in anguish to Bruno Walter:

> I must alter my whole way of life. You cannot imagine how painful this is to me. For years I have grown used to taking strenuous exercise, to walking in forests and over mountains and boldly wresting my ideas from nature. I would sit at my desk only as a peasant brings in his harvest, to give shape to my sketches. Even my spiritual worries disappeared after a long walk or a climb. Now I must avoid all effort, watch myself constantly, walk as little as possible. Living, as I do here, in solitude and concentrating on myself, I feel more intensely all that's wrong with me physically. Perhaps I'm looking on the black side, but since I've been in the countryside I've felt less well than in town, where distractions kept my mind occupied.

Alma described this as 'the saddest summer' they spent together:

> We were afraid of everything. He was always stopping on a walk to feel his pulse and he often asked me to listen to his heart and see whether the beat was clear or rapid or calm. I had often implored him to give up his long bicycle rides, his climbing and swimming under

water, to which he was so passionately attached. There was nothing of
that now. On the contrary he had a pedometer in his pocket. His steps
and pulse-beats were numbered and his life a torment. Every excursion,
every attempt at distraction was a failure.[1]

Walter evidently suggested some psychological reason for
Mahler's despondency. He received a dusty answer:

What is all this nonsense about the soul and its sickness? And where
should I go to cure it? ... To find myself I need to be here alone. Since
I've been seized by this panic I have tried to direct my eyes and ears
elsewhere, but to rediscover myself, I have got to accept the horrors of
loneliness. . . . I have in no sense a hypochondriac's fear of death, as
you suppose. I have always known I must die ... but all at once I have
lost the serenity and confidence I had acquired. . . . As far as my 'work'
is concerned, it is most depressing to have to unlearn everything. I
have never been able to work only at my desk—I need outside exercise
for my inner exercises. . . . After a gentle little walk my pulse beats so
fast and I feel so oppressed that I don't even achieve the desired effect
of forgetting my body. . . . This is the greatest calamity I have ever
known.

His salvation, in the end, was more-than-usual absorption in
the Bethge songs he had begun in the previous summer. *Die
chinesische Flöte* was one more manifestation of the fashion for
orientalism which spread throughout the arts of this period
(Busoni's *Turandot* and Puccini's *Madama Butterfly* are two
musical examples). The poems entranced him and matched his
mood. He had intended to call the new song-cycle *Die Flöte aus
Jade* (*The Jade Flute*) but he changed it to *Das Lied von Jammer
der Erde* (*The Song of Earth's Sorrow*). Finally, he extended it
by insertion of orchestral interludes into a new kind of work, a
song-symphony which he eventually entitled *Das Lied von der
Erde* (*Song of the Earth*). By 1st September the sixth song was
completed in short score. His visitors found him an altered man:

[1] A. Mahler, *Gustav Mahler*, op. cit.

he had regained his calm and found a new delight in nature. To Walter he wrote: 'I was full of zeal (and you will thus realize that I have now become "acclimatized") ... I believe this is quite the most personal thing I have done.'

The summer ended with a visit to Prague to conduct the first performance of the Seventh Symphony on 19th September. Many young musicians went there to hear the rehearsals, among them Alban Berg, Otto Klemperer, Gabrilovitch and Bodanzky. Mahler was 'torn by doubts' about the work and spent hours revising the orchestration and himself altering all the orchestral parts—it was, after all, three years since he had completed it. It was during a rehearsal for woodwind and brass alone that a remark was made which enabled Mahler, writing to Alma on 10th September, to make a famous analogy:

One of the trumpeters asked Bodanzky in despair: 'I'd just like to know what's beautiful about blowing away at a trumpet stopped up to high C sharp.' This made me think deeply about the lot of man, who also cannot understand why he must endure being 'stopped' to the piercing agony of his own existence, cannot see what it's for, and how his screech is to be attuned to the great harmony of the universal symphony of all creation.

Always the philosopher! The symphony had a respectful, puzzled reception.

Returning from New York in the spring of 1909, Mahler sat to Rodin in Paris for a bust. At Toblach, in June, he was on his own, for Alma was ill, her nerves 'in a critical state'. Much is said about Mahler's neuroses, but the reader of Alma's memoirs cannot fail to notice the hypertension of her own personality, the constant references to her fainting-fits and 'heart attacks'. She cannot have been easy to live with. Mahler at this time was taking pains to 'make peace' with people with whom he had quarrelled. 'It gives me the deepest satisfaction ... to love as long as I still can love', he told Alma. She went to Levico and

Mahler stayed with friends at Göding. He was at work on the Ninth Symphony:

I feel marvellous here! To be able to sit working by the open window, and breathing the air, the trees and flowers all the time—this is a delight I have never known till now. I see now how perverse my life in summer has always been. I feel myself getting better every minute. I shudder when I think of my various 'workshops'; although I have spent the happiest hours of my life in them, it has probably been at the price of my health.

This mood of optimism had developed while he was in New York earlier in the year, when he had written to Walter:

My life is so infinitely full of experiences (since a year and a half ago) [i.e. July 1907]. I can hardly talk about it. How should I attempt to describe so appalling a crisis! I see everything in a new light—feel so much alive, and the habit of being alive is sweeter than ever. I should not be surprised at times if suddenly I should notice that I had a new body (like Faust in the last scene) . . . .How foolish it is . . . to be untrue even for a short hour to oneself and to the higher things above us. . . . Strange! When I hear music—even while I conduct—I can hear quite definite answers to all my questions and feel entirely clear and sure. Or rather, I feel quite clearly that they are not questions at all.

He was elated by the performances of his Seventh Symphony by the Concertgebouw of Amsterdam (3rd and 7th October) which he conducted before sailing to New York. 'The orchestra . . . said they wanted so much to learn Beethoven and Wagner from me. . . . When you have to work really hard, it is living.' There is no suggestion here, or in the music he was writing, of a man cringing under the shadow of death. They returned to Europe in the spring of 1910 and again went to Paris, where Mahler conducted his Second Symphony. Debussy, Dukas and Pierné left during the second movement. Too Schubertian, they are said to have explained. But the public and critics liked it. Thence to Rome, where Mahler, alerted to the incompetence of the orchestra by Mengelberg, violently abused the players, who walked out of rehearsal and adopted a policy of non-co-operation at the concert.

Mahler and Alma then returned to Vienna and to Toblach for their summer routine. But this time it was to be different. Since the dreadful month of July 1907 Alma had been far from well. The strain of coping with Mahler's new régime of life drove her to the brink of a breakdown, in which there was a strong element of sexual frustration. She went in May for a rest-cure to a sanatorium at Tobeldad where the doctor, worried by her despondency, prescribed dancing. Thus she met a hand-some architect four years her junior, Walter Gropius, who soon declared his love for her and hoped for its reciprocation. Mahler was working on his Tenth Symphony and was also preoccupied with preliminary rehearsals for the vast undertaking of the first performance of the Eighth Symphony, scheduled for Munich in September. His letters are full of illuminating comments on the difficulties involved. When he visited Alma at Tobeldad he was struck by her radiance: 'When I told you how nice you looked, it was the expression of a spontaneous delight,' he solemnly wrote. 'I live only for you and Gucki.' Gropius wrote to Alma in July saying he could not live without her and inviting her to leave Mahler and go to him. By accident, so he later maintained, he addressed the envelope to 'Herr Direktor Mahler'. In what followed Alma at last told Mahler of all she had sacrificed for him.

At this point, Alma says, Mahler realized his own guilt. She was thirty and beautiful, still rejoicing in her attractiveness to men. Gabrilovitch, for example, had declared his love before they first sailed for America. Mahler's idea of a happy family evening was for Alma to read Eschenbach's *Parsifal* aloud or Lange's *Geschichte des Materialismus*, and to discuss lectures on astronomy which she attended at his behest. 'You have an abstraction for a husband,' a friend told her. Not only were her sexual needs unfulfilled, she was starved of fun too. Now, in this crisis, she still kept something back: 'I knew that my marriage was no marriage and that my own life was utterly unfulfilled. I concealed all this from him, and although he knew it as well as I did we played out the comedy to the end.'

The bedroom intimacies of a marriage concern only the people involved, but Alma throughout her books drops hints like someone laying a paper trail. Whatever Mahler's weaknesses of the flesh, she did not intend that they should perish with him in 1911. If she means us to believe that he was intermittently impotent, then her book suggests she feared that his physical powers would be restored every time his old flame Anna von Mildenburg visited them. Whereas Alma, by her own admission, was highly sexed, it is likely that Mahler was one of those men for whom intellectual creative work, in his case composing and conducting, reduces and sublimates sexual drive. On the other hand, there is Ida Dehmel's impression of him in 1905: 'He is the first Jew except my father to impress me as a man—one who doesn't, to put it crudely, strike me as impotent.' [2] No doubt the crisis of 1908, when he became obsessed with the need to conserve his physical energies, affected him sexually. Perhaps by 1910 he was impotent or so disinclined for intercourse that Alma was ripe for the attentions of Gropius.

Gropius followed her to Toblach in July. Mahler insisted she should meet him and himself brought Gropius to the house, ordering her to choose between them. 'Almschili,' he wrote to her some weeks later, 'if you had left me that time, I should simply have gone out like a torch deprived of air.' She wrote in her book on Mahler:

I could never have imagined life without him . . . least of all could I have imagined life with another man. I had often thought of going away somewhere alone to start life afresh, but never with any thought of another person. Mahler was the hub of my existence.

[2] Quoted in A. Mahler, *Gustav Mahler*, op. cit.

'He loved humanity but he often forgot man,' Walter said of him. Women too. But during this time he found Alma's compositions, which she had kept since they were married. 'What have I done?' he said, and encouraged her to revise them. That was one frustration eased. He became as devoted and submissive to her as he had formerly been tyrannical. (And it is distasteful, reading between the lines of Alma's book, to realize that she relished the sense of power, at any rate for a time. One suspects she enjoyed crises.) He wrote loving notes to her while she slept and left them by her bed. His guilt sent him to a neurologist, who sent him to Freud in August. Whether Freud was of any help or whether he further distressed Mahler is arguable.

This painfully intimate episode has been fully related, not only because it led directly to Mahler's consultation with Freud but because we have further visible evidence of his agony of mind during the crisis in the messages to Alma which he wrote on the manuscript of the Tenth Symphony. 'Farewell my lyre. . . . you alone know the meaning of this. . . . Almschili, to live for you, to die for you. . . . Have mercy, O Lord, why hast thou forsaken me?' The man was in a private hell, near to delirium. During this summer he reached his fiftieth birthday. 'I know if you were in Vienna now, you would be so warmly wrapped in honour that you might forget all your earlier and fully justified resentments,' Schoenberg wrote. A month later Mahler lent a large sum to Schoenberg, who was in financial distress. He also agreed to forgo profits on the publication of his first four symphonies so that Universal Edition could take over Bruckner's works.

The first performance of the Eighth Symphony meant even more to Mahler now for, as a thanksgiving, he had offered Alma the dedication. 'Does it not make the impression of a betrothal?' he wrote to her in one of the many passionate and almost painfully moving love-letters which poured from him, the last of them containing these poignant words: 'For the first time for

73

eight weeks—in my whole life, for that matter—I feel the bliss-
ful happiness love gives to one who, loving with all his soul,
knows he is loved in return. After all, my dream has come true:
"I lost the world, but found my harbour!"' A few days before
the performance he developed a septic throat and high tempera-
ture, but recovered in time for the final rehearsal—'Every note
addressed to you'—and the performances on 12th and 13th
September. Despite signs of physical fatigue he secured a triumphant realization of his immense creation. The audience acclaimed him like a god. He did not conduct in Europe again.

The septic throat and accompanying fever returned in New
York at Christmas and in February, when he was compelled to
abandon the last part of his Philharmonic season. Joseph Fränkel,
their New York doctor, realized the fatal nature of the illness
and ordered blood tests which showed a streptococcal infection.
Mahler's malady of subacute bacterial endocarditis occurs in
hearts which have a congenital or acquired valvular lesion. In
his case it was almost certainly acquired; this can be caused by
rheumatic fever or syphilis or repeated streptococcal sore throats.
There is no evidence of the first two where Mahler was concerned,
but plenty of the last. Today penicillin would have saved him.

His condition fluctuated from day to day. He could still joke
with Alma: 'You will be in great demand when I am gone. Now
who shall it be?' He named the candidates. 'It'll be better, after
all, if I stay with you.' Fränkel advised his return to Paris to see
a bacteriologist: Paris at that time was the centre for the study
of bacteria serums following Pasteur's discoveries. They sailed
early in April. In Paris he saw André Chantemesse, of the Pasteur
Institute. He grew weaker, rallied feverishly, relapsed. He read
philosophy—Hartmann's *The Problem of Life*—as he had
always done. He planned a holiday in Egypt when he was better.
But he did not compose. When his condition worsened Alma
sent for the Viennese blood specialist, Franz Chvostek, who
ordered him to a Vienna sanatorium. There he lay, surrounded

by flowers, sometimes lucid, sometimes delirious. He saw old friends, like Walter and Berliner. Walter found him gloomy, forbidding and pessimistic in mood, showing annoyance at the mention of what was going on in Vienna's musical life but anxious to hear about old friends. He worried what would happen to Schoenberg. He entrusted the sketches of his Tenth Symphony to Alma's care and discretion. As uraemia set in and he passed from consciousness he said, again and again, 'My Almschi,' and sometimes, 'Mozart'. On 18th May 1911 he died, like Beethoven, during a thunderstorm. He was aged fifty years and forty-six weeks. 'No doubt he will now become a great man in Vienna too,' said Richard Strauss.[3] As he had wished, he was buried beside his daughter Putzi in the Vienna suburb of Grinzing. He had asked too for nothing but the name 'Gustav Mahler 'on the headstone. 'Any who come to look for me will know who I was, and the rest do not need to know.'

[3] Letter to Hofmannsthal, 20th May 1911.

9 Characteristics

The tendency for discussion of Mahler's music to move into realms of philosophical and psychological verbiage is perhaps familiar to readers. His music lends itself easily to extra-musical analysis, indeed it is among the most autobiographical music ever written, and to pretend that it exists only in terms of musical procedures is to miss an element which Mahler explicitly commanded us to take into account. Each of his symphonies is an extension of his personality, an exploration of himself, and in his case, as in Elgar's and Berlioz's, it is not possible—in fact it is wrong—to separate the music from the life of its composer as though it was an isolated activity. At the same time one must guard against a too-literal association of life and music and make due allowance for the creative imagination.

Because of the tragi-romantic course of Mahler's life, in particular the shadow hanging over it from 1907 to its end, too much emphasis has been laid on the obsession with death and the long farewell. The picture of Mahler as doom-laden, neurotically introspective, temperamentally unbalanced, while not a total misrepresentation, is a distortion of the reality. True, his music derives its greatness from the conflicts and contradictions of his personality: the man of action (as he was) and the man who needed, as he told Alma, to be 'often and intensely alone'; the philosopher and quasi-scientist and the simple-hearted child of nature. The music does not bear out an interpretation of Mahler as a gloomy life-denier: he was positive, affirmatory. Most of the symphonies are joyous and life-giving, whatever struggles they may record. Only the Sixth ends in the minor.

We should beware, too, of the fashion for relating Mahler's music to such vague but imposing concepts as 'a microcosm of the decay of Western society'. It is tempting to be wise after the event and find hints and portents of impending dissolution and destruction in this music, even spurious relevances to the events of today. But it is Gustav Mahler who is in these symphonies in microcosm, not Western society and its political evolution and revolution. The Left are naturally anxious to claim him for their own—a man of the people, bringing the music of the people into his own art. Of course he did: most great creative artists are humanitarians. In 1905, Alma records, he met a workers' May Day procession in the Ring in Vienna and accompanied it for some distance. 'They had all looked at him in so brotherly a way—they *were* his brothers—and they were the future!' If some of these brothers had turned up next day in the Vienna Opera chorus, they would soon have discovered how far Mahler's fraternal instincts went in practice. But it is true to say that he democratized the symphony, or rather that he gave it back its Beethovenian democracy. (It is also true that he belonged to a Vienna Socialist-vegetarian group in 1880.)

The use in his symphonies of waltzes, *Ländler*, marches and snatches of song was his practical means of fulfilling his creed that 'the symphony is the world, it must embrace everything'. For a man of his philosophical cast of mind the symphony was the obvious medium. Restricted to a few months' composing in a year, Mahler had no time for concertos and other forms, but even if he had had time I doubt if he would have chosen otherwise. The symphony was his *Wunderhorn* of plenty, and he fertilized it from the great Austro-German tradition of song. It was his chosen vessel for self-expression, as music-drama was Wagner's and the mazurka Chopin's. It is ironically amusing to consider Vaughan Williams's famous backhanded compliment to Mahler—'intimate acquaintance with the executive side of

77

music . . . made even Mahler into a very tolerable imitation of a composer' [1]—when one considers how fully Mahler fulfils Vaughan Williams's creative ideal: 'Have we not all about us forms of musical expression which we can purify and raise to the level of great art? . . . We must cultivate a sense of musical citizenship.' [2] This applies as much to the Mahler of the Third Symphony as it does to the composer of *A London Symphony*. Among English composers Elgar may be psychologically nearest to Mahler, but Vaughan Williams's symphonies are Mahlerian in ethos, if in nothing else. Mahler and Vaughan Williams erected imposing and inspiring structures often on unpromising material. They stretched the symphony to wider terms of reference—not to mention the bond of folksong, so despised by Elgar.

Admirers of Mahler's music give three principal reasons for their enthusiasm: his melodic gift, his mastery of form, and his originality of sound (in other words, his brilliance as an orchestrator). The second has had to be defended strongly. The size of Mahler's symphonies makes them for some people synonymous with sprawl. But he needed a vast canvas on which to work out the intricate relationship of his themes, for it cannot be denied that his symphonies are complex. Their length is in proportion to their material. The allegation that he was a natural song-writer who mistakenly attempted to write symphonies shows a lack of understanding comparable with Bernard Shaw's strictures on Schubert for lack of 'head-work'.

The unmistakable 'Mahler sound' principally derives from his superb orchestral mastery—I say principally, because there is a certain shape, a tone of voice, in the very outline of a Mahler melody that proclaims its origin even on the pianoforte. Here

[1] R. Vaughan Williams, *Musical Autobiography*, which first appeared in Hubert Foss, *Ralph Vaughan Williams* (London, 1950).

[2] R. Vaughan Williams, *Who Wants the English Composer?* (London, 1912).

again one discovers when one listens attentively to Mahler how mistaken was the old assertion that his music was an overblown, decadent swan song of Wagnerian Romanticism. Mahler's textures are often bare and stark, in spite of the very large orchestra he used. Partly his need for such large forces was determined by the dynamic contrasts necessary in the huge dimensions of his symphonic movements. Partly too it was dictated by his unceasing search for clarity above all else: the chief characteristic, also, of his conducting. Mahler's music is in reaction to the full orchestral textures of Wagnerian sound. His scores contain comparatively few *tutti*—though when he wants a *fortissimo* he can create a tremendous one—and are full of solos: for horn, flute, oboe, E♭ clarinet, trumpet—all instruments with a very clear-cut sound. His enlargement of the woodwind department promoted it symphonically to the status of strings and brass. His writing for strings rarely has the comfortable, luxuriant 'richness' of Wagner and Bruckner: again, it is the insistence on exposed, clear part-writing. The result is that Mahler's orchestra can aptly be compared to a vast chamber orchestra, most memorably in *Das Lied von der Erde*, but in the earliest works too. In this connection it is instructive to quote his words to Natalie Bauer-Lechner in 1896: 'I never use the middle strings where passionate expression is required, they do not sound right. They are more suitable for soft, veiled and mysterious parts.' He was above all the pioneer of a *concertante* style of writing for the modern symphony orchestra which has been carried to extreme lengths by composers working fifty years after his death. He pioneered too the range of colour to be obtained from the percussion.

Paramount concern with clarity led Mahler to highly detailed markings of dynamics in his scores and to sometimes lengthy printed adjurations to his interpreters. As a conductor he well knew orchestras' deficiencies and the difficulties of his own scores. Yet an intelligent English critic, Mr Desmond Shawe-Taylor, has written [3] that 'Mahler was hysterical, in fact neurotic to a high degree, as could be deduced without hearing a note of the music merely from the frenzied anxiety of his markings and instructions to the conductor'. Poor Mahler, the supreme professional: in some English eyes he cannot win. But the strange thing is that his intimate and profound practical knowledge of the orchestra did not give him absolute certainty of achieving his intentions. He was an inveterate reviser, the Fourth, Fifth, Sixth and Seventh Symphonies being subjected to constant alterations, not all of which are yet incorporated into published scores. The process of creation was for him never 'finished', in either sense of the word. During rehearsals of the Eighth Symphony at Munich in 1910 he turned to some of the musicians in the audience and said: 'If, after my death, something doesn't sound right, then change it. You have not only the right but the duty to do so.' [4]

The fundamental principle in Mahler's technique of composition was two-part counterpoint. This was a natural means for his expression of what lies at the root of all his work: conflict. Conflict is not satisfactorily conveyed by melody cushioned by changing harmonies. For Mahler the essence of his style seems to have been associated with the use of bare intervals, fourths and fifths, and pedal-points. As he developed, and as his scoring became ever more sinewy, he abandoned pedal-points so that his two-part contrapuntal form became detached from the conventional sense of tonality, with each part independent of the other and liable to separate development, as in the Ninth Symphony (Ex. 1 opposite).

To the ordinary listener and concert-goer the outstanding features of Mahler's achievement are his convincing incorporation into his immense structures of the everyday sounds which had so potent an emotional effect upon him. It is here that he is

[3] *Sunday Times*, 17th September 1972.
[4] P. Heyworth (ed.), *Conversations with Klemperer* (London, 1973), p. 34.

a truly revolutionary composer who took an established form, symphony, and gave it new and fruitful life. For example, there is the folksong element, as found in the tune from the *Lieder eines fahrenden Gesellen* which is used again in Symphony No. 1:

Then there is Mahler's ability to give a deliberately vulgar tune a frightening twist, rather as if some childhood memory of a fairground had been shadowed by the cruelty of a Punch-and-Judy episode (also from the First Symphony):

Ex. 3

Like Bach and Bruckner—and, later, Berg and others—Mahler knew the power of a hymn-like tune (chorale) at crucial moments, as in the Symphony No. 2:

Ex. 4

Then, antedating Skriabin, Messiaen and even Delius, he exploited in the most poetic manner imitations of the calls of birds—his cuckoo in Symphony No. 1 calls in the interval of a fourth—lending a mystical sense of loneliness to the music. This device reached its highest artistic point in *Das Lied von der Erde*. He produces similar emotional and dramatic effect from the continual use of march tunes and rhythms, as in this example from Symphony No. 3:

Ex. 5

Other pervasive fingerprints are the use of *Ländler* dance-tunes and the impressive atmosphere created by such simple yet imaginative touches as horns calling to each other across a valley (Symphony No. 5) and the cow-bells episode in Symphony No. 6.

Some discussion of Mahler's musical ancestry is inevitable, although the hunting down of 'influences' on such a personal composer is even less helpful than usual. Allied to this there is the problem, if such it be, of his eclecticism. Most composers are eclectic: they borrow from each other, they imitate the same models. It matters little as long as they can impart their own personality to what they borrow. Again one may call Vaughan Williams to Mahler's defence: 'Why should music be original? ... The duty of the composer is to find the *mot juste*. It does not matter if this word has been said a thousand times before as long as it is the right thing to say at that moment.' Mahler's genius as a conductor must have contributed towards his eclecticism: it was impossible for a man who sank himself so deeply into the works of others not to absorb subconsciously their spirit and sometimes their letter.

Mahler belongs to the symphonic lineage of Haydn, Schubert, Beethoven and Bruckner. He often has a Haydnesque pastoral flavour; like Schubert he imparted the breadth of strophic song to symphonic thinking; he emulated Beethoven in awareness of humanity and humanity's aspirations; like Bruckner, he worked best over a huge span, with room to move and time to breathe. But to none of these did he owe as much in substance as he did to Berlioz, whose masterly and unconventional way of handling a symphony, as in the *Fantastique* with its waltz, march, pastoral scene and witches' round dance, was obviously etched into Mahler's mind as ineradicably as his clear and colourful orchestration. Much as he admired Wagner for his thematic development, there is little of Wagner in Mahler, who saw clearly that Wagner represented an impasse. Though he is often linked with Bruckner, they inhabit different spiritual atmospheres. Superficial resemblances exist, but to experience the dissimilarity of Bruckner and Mahler one has only to listen to an *adagio* by each. A Bruckner *adagio* cannot progress beyond a few bars before we feel we are being lifted into another world; a Mahler *adagio* is inescapably of this world. Even when Mahler raises his eyes to heaven seeking redemption, even when he is 'lost to the world', he is shackled to it by his sense of mortality. Sometimes, as in the Fourth Symphony, there is peace of a sort, a spiritual armistice, but the tension of the counterpoint remains. It has been well said that Mahler was always looking for God, but Bruckner had found Him. Strauss never began the search.

Mahler's wife and several of his friends, notably Schoenberg, described him as a saint. They did not mean, we may be sure, any effete, stained-glass saint. Saints are toughened by suffering; they are men of steel, stoics, lashed by the world and their own sense of sin. Of this company was Mahler; and in exploring his work this steeliness of purpose and strength of fibre should not be overlooked.

10 Songs and Symphony No. 1

Mahler's earliest works need not detain us for more than a few lines. Some have already been mentioned. Mahler told Natalie Bauer-Lechner:

At the Conservatoire I never finished a single score. I usually stopped after the first or second movement, occasionally after the third . . . not because I was impatient to start another but because, before even finishing my work, I was no longer satisfied with it. I had already moved beyond it.

Some of the earliest compositions which he allowed to be published are in the three books of *Lieder und Gesänge aus der Jugendzeit* (Songs from the Days of Youth). The first of the three books, all published in 1892, comprises five songs written between 1880 and 1883. The remaining books contain nine settings from *Des Knaben Wunderhorn*, which will be considered in that context. Of Book I, the third song, *Hans und Grethe*, to a text by Mahler, was composed on 5th March 1880 as one of a proposed set of five songs dedicated to Josephine Poisl, daughter of the postmaster at Iglau, of which three survived. It was originally called *Maitanz im Grünen*. It is a delightful song and is important because it is Mahler's first use of the *Ländler* dance-rhythm and also because it became the main theme of the *scherzo* of the First Symphony, the first example of Mahler's thematic linking of song and symphony. *Erinnerung* is even more prophetic, the first highly organized example of the type of melancholy song in which Mahler excelled. *Frühlingsmorgen*, wistful and animated,

belongs to the *Lied* as understood by Schumann. Two settings
of texts from Tirso de Molina's *Don Juan*, the *Serenade* and *Phantasie*, are pleasant folkish songs, noteworthy because they provide
a clue to Mahler's natural inclination to think of his accompaniments in orchestral terms. He recommends a harp as the accompaniment to *Phantasie*, and the *Serenade* is subtitled 'with
accompaniment by wind instruments', although no score has
come to light.

Roughly contemporary with the first five *Lieder und Gesänge*
—the chronology of Mahler's early works is still far from having
been established definitively—is the large-scale cantata *Das
klagende Lied* (*The Song of Sorrow*). Mahler followed Wagner's
practice by writing the libretto before composing the music. He
completed the text on 18th March 1878 and the music of the
original three-part version on 1st November 1880. Mahler
adapted the text from a story in an anthology of folk-tales published in 1856 by Ludwig Bechstein.[1] He introduced certain
variations taken from a Grimm tale *Der singende Knochen* (*The
Singing Bone*) which appeared in 1870. In Mahler's poem—
written in the *Wunderhorn* style—a queen offers herself in
marriage to the man who shall find a certain red flower. Two
brothers search for it. The younger finds it, puts it in his hat and
lies down to sleep. The elder brother discovers him, kills him,
takes the flower and buries him beneath a willow tree. He claims
his bride. In Part II the minstrel (*Der Spielmann*) finds a bone
under the willow tree. He makes it into a flute. When he plays
it, the 'flute' tells of his murder by his brother. In Part III the
minstrel arrives at the castle on the queen's wedding day. He
plays the flute, which again repeats the story of murder. The king
seizes the flute and puts it to his lips; the 'singing bone' then
accuses him: 'Oh brother, it was you who murdered me.' The
queen collapses, the guests run away and the castle begins to

[1] *Neues deutsches Märchenbuch* (Leipzig and Pesth). No. 3 is *Das klagende Lied*.

fall to the ground. It is worth noting that in the Bechstein tale a brother and sister are involved. Mahler substituted two brothers, and this has been linked by some writers, not implausibly, with his feelings of guilt that he had been spared while his beloved younger brother Ernst had died in 1874.

The musical history of *Das klagende Lied* is complicated. Some writers have said it was originally planned as an opera, but this seems to be unlikely because there is no documentary—and not much musical—evidence for the theory. The three parts of the first version were entitled *Waldmärchen* (Forest Legend), *Der Spielmann* and *Hochzeitstück* (Wedding Piece). This version was not performed in Mahler's lifetime. Having failed to win the Beethoven Prize with it in 1881, he left it untouched until September 1893 in Hamburg, when he excised Part I. The revised version, therefore, comprises only *Der Spielmann* and *Hochzeitstück*. It was published in 1902 and first performed on 17th February 1901 in Vienna, conducted by Mahler. The score of *Waldmärchen* was kept by Mahler's sister Justine, who bequeathed it to her son, Alfred Rosé. He conducted it on Radio Brno in 1934, and conducted the complete original version on Vienna Radio the following year. Nothing further occurred until the score was bought by Thomas and Marshall Osborn of New Haven, Connecticut, in 1969, enabling the first public performance to be given in New Haven in January 1970.

The original version has been recorded by Pierre Boulez, a convinced champion of this cantata. It remains a puzzle why Mahler should have discarded *Waldmärchen*. It cannot have been because of length: he was soon to write longer compositions. Musically and dramatically this first section is essential to the shape and atmosphere of the work. Its orchestral opening is magnificent, the key of A minor imbued with that mystery and tension which always surround it in Mahler. The horn-calls tell us that this young composer knows his early Wagner: but the oboe and other woodwind tell us that his name is Mahler.

Das klagende Lied largely retains interest today—it is no master-piece, and to insist that it is merely devalues his later achievements—because of its flashes of the real Mahler. Already there is the clarity, though rarely the pungency, of the mature scoring; there is the gift for broad-spanned melody, such as the serene passage describing the young man's death, 'Der Junge lächelt wie im Traum' (the youth smiles as if in a dream); there is the mastery in handling a large design. Most significant from this point of view are the use and recurrence of orchestral interludes which develop the material and carry the drama a stage further, just as they do in *Das Lied von der Erde*. Indeed it becomes tedious to point out the foreshadowings of later works in the early works, the predilection for a falling fourth, the major-minor modulations: they will be obvious to attuned listeners. Suffice it to say that certain musical shapes (images) were intuitive to Mahler and give his music an organic unity carrying over from one work to the next. He was a very consistent composer. The one really operatic section of the cantata is in Part III, the wedding scene, where the opening set-piece for orchestra and chorus seems to belong to the theatre, as does the strikingly effective use of an off-stage wind band—Mahler's first use of a deliberately vulgar thematic contrast. The Hoffmannesque world of the romantic novel is the milieu of *Das klagende Lied*. Its weakness lies in its too obvious derivation from Weber and Wagner and in the comparatively staid writing for the chorus and the soloists. Only the soprano has a really exciting part, containing some extravagant vocal leaps. But the reason that the cantata fails to grip the listener as much as it might is, I think, that it is too objective. The tragedy happens to someone else, not to Mahler himself, and neither he nor we feel sufficiently involved.

What Mahler learned from practical experience in the four years between the completion of *Das klagende Lied* and the composition in 1884 of the song-cycle *Lieder eines fahrenden*

Gesellen is obvious from the first orchestral sounds of the latter,
even allowing for the revisions which he made in his prime.
There is still no certainty whether the 'Wayfarer' song-cycle
was conceived for orchestra or pianoforte accompaniment, but
reliable evidence suggests orchestration in 1892–3. Written
as a memorial to the affair with Johanna Richter, the 'Wayfarer'
cycle is in the tradition of Schubert's *Winterreise*, the same
tradition that led in English music to Vaughan Williams's *Songs
of Travel*. In the first song Mahler's wanderer, on his sweetheart's
wedding day, contrasts the loveliness of nature with his own
grief. As he walks through the fields, in the second song, the
birds and flowers greet him, but his heart cannot respond. In the
third song the girl's blue eyes haunt him so that he wishes he
were dead. These eyes drive him, in the last song, into the world
lonely and sad—a funeral march in E minor, a semitone higher
than the ending of the previous song. But under a lime tree he
sleeps and forgets his grief—a passage moving from F major
into the minor and similar to the Young Knight's death under
the willow in *Das klagende Lied*. But this time we know the
wanderer is Mahler himself. The *Gesellen* songs constitute a
masterpiece because they still sound original, fresh and evolutionary—only Berlioz's *Les Nuits d'Été* can compare with them
in this respect. Mahler perfectly reconciles the simple folk-like
lilt of his vocal tunes with the sophisticated tone-painting of the
accompaniment. The use of tonality is startlingly unorthodox, as
it was always to be. Keys are roughly and illogically contrasted.
The cycle begins in D minor, and ends in F minor after experi-
encing F♯ minor, B major and E minor. The music, for all its
attractive tunefulness, has a sharp edge, verging on bitter irony,
which is far more characteristic of Mahler than sentimentality.
The scoring is light, almost impressionistic.

The song-cycle is intimately connected, thematically and
emotionally, with the Symphony No. 1 in D, the two together
making a remarkable autobiographical commentary on Mahler's

youth. Since there are cross-references also in the symphony to *Das klagende Lied*, the songs and another work, it will be seen that these works must be taken together, with the symphony as the summing-up. This was no doubt why Mahler first described the symphony as a symphonic poem: he could have called it 'The Wayfarer', because it follows the plan of the song-cycle. The blithe second song, *Ging heut' Morgen übers Feld* becomes the principal theme of the first movement, and the gentle epilogue of the fourth song reappears in the slow movement. Not only that, but the opening of the rustic *scherzo* derives from the song *Hans und Grethe*, a cross-reference to the affair with Josephine Poisl. Another of the songs dedicated to her, *Im Lenz*, is used in *Das klagende Lied*:

Ex. 6

The symphony, then, is a love story; but Mahler, in a letter to Max Marschalk dated 26th March 1896, explains not only that but his attitude to the then burning question of programme music (and, incidentally, why he disapproved of analytical notes):

I would like to have it stressed that the symphony is greater than the love affair it is based on, or rather it preceded it as far as the emotional life of the creator is concerned. The real affair became the reason for, but by no means the real meaning of, the work. . . . My need to express my feelings in music in a symphony begins only where the mysterious feelings take over at the gate which leads into the 'other world', a world which does not separate happenings through time or space. Just as I find it a platitude to invent music to fit a programme, I find it sterile to give a programme for a completed work. The fact that the inspiration or basis of a composition is an experience of its author does not alter things.

In 1967 the original five-movement score of the First Symphony came to light, including the short second movement which Mahler eliminated before publication in 1899. This was a delicately scored *Andante* entitled *Blumine*, and it was a remnant of the incidental music Mahler wrote for *Der Trompeter von Säkkingen*, where it did duty as a 'moonlight serenade on the trumpet blown across the Rhine'. Mahler not only incorporated it into the symphony but made it an integral part of the work by quoting it in the finale. His abandonment of it, for whatever reason, again seems to me to be a mistake both for itself—it is beautiful—and for its place in the structure. Without *Blumine* the second subject of the finale seems to have no function in that movement: it is just a luscious tune. But when *Blumine* has been included the whole point of recalling the theme in this form becomes apparent (Ex. 7 opposite).

One can understand why the symphony was so unpopular in Mahler's lifetime only when one remembers how bizarre its orchestration must have sounded. Audiences were uncomfortable with the touches of *grotesquerie* in the otherwise benignly lyrical slow movement, the Callot-inspired funeral procession of the huntsman accompanied to his grave by forest animals, all to a parody of the popular round *Bruder Martin* (or *Frère Jacques*). But this picturesque Romantic work belongs to the world of Dvořák and Tchaikovsky. Its beautiful opening, depicting a spring dawn, with birdsong and cuckoo-calls, is a vivid and imaginative piece of nature-painting; the *Ländler-scherzo* is a Mahlerian version of the Austrian peasant dance-forms hallowed by Bruckner and Haydn—it is the latter's spirit which predominates. Perhaps the triumphant climax of the finale (with horn-players ordered to stand) is too blatantly

Ex. 7

stage-managed after the recall of the first movement dawn-music, but it will be actively disliked only by those who cringe at Elgar's revised ending of the *Enigma Variations*. Today this revolutionary masterpiece is a popular work; yet its first Vienna performance on 19th November 1900 ended in pande-monium. What hurt Mahler most was that the Philharmonic Orchestra, 'which is able to understand my work better than anyone else, deserted me at the end of the concert. The musicians positively rejoiced at the fiasco and averted their faces to hide the malice in their eyes'. Thus Vienna once again maltreated genius.

Somewhere, perhaps, are the scores of apprentice works which would show Mahler's journey towards the maturity shown in this symphony, especially his mastery of by far the largest orchestra used in a symphony up to that date. The organic unity of the work, achieved by thematic cross-reference (and therefore strengthened by the inclusion of *Blumine*) and the employment of a progressive scheme of tonality, indicate the distance travelled by Mahler in eight years. It marked the end of the beginning.

Not the least of Mahler's achievements in these years was his reconstruction of Weber's comic opera *Die drei Pintos*, of which sketches for only seven numbers existed at the time of Weber's death in 1826, together with bare indications for instrumentation of only a very few bars. By using these sketches, composing new sections based on the themes they contained, and skilfully incor-porating other music by Weber, Mahler extended the opera to twenty-one numbers and restored a delightful work to the stage. In the orchestral entr'acte and in other anachronistic touches of scoring, the Mahler of the First Symphony can easily be detected, but the remarkable feature of this posthumous collaboration is its fidelity to the spirit of Weber.

11 *Wunderhorn* Symphonies

The Second, Third and Fourth Symphonies are usually classified as the *Wunderhorn* symphonies because of their links with Mahler's settings of poems from *Das Knaben Wunderhorn*. This could apply equally to the First Symphony, for the words of *Das klagende Lied* and the *Gesellen* cycle are Mahler's pastiche of the *Wunderhorn* poems, proving how deeply embedded in his mind were the style and spirit of the anthology.

Mahler's first settings of *Wunderhorn* poems were for voice and pianoforte, although obviously conceived for orchestral accompaniment, and were written in the late 1880s. Twelve more, originally entitled *Humoresken*, date from 1892 to 1901. They alternate between a charming fairy-tale delicacy and a grimly ironic, nightmarish realization and interpenetration of the moods of military bluster and nocturnal mystery. They are outstanding for the quivering sensitivity of the composer's response to the text of each poem and, once again, for the beauty and aptness of sound with which this response is matched. The cornerstones of Mahler's style were cross-reference, variation and development, and even in such small-scale works as the songs the constant change enacted gives them a scope beyond the ordinary. Even in such an overtly simple and 'innocent' (though seductive) song as *Rheinlegendchen*, the range of tonality beyond the nominal home key of A major is remarkable. In *Das irdische Leben* the development by means of major-minor contrasts gives the song its psychological depth. Mahler's exploitation of contrast, his genius for savage juxtapositions, can be heard at their starkest in the 'duologue' *Wunderhorn* songs such as *Der Schildwache Nachtlied*.

The finest and most significant of the songs are what may be called the 'military nocturnes', where trumpet-calls, march rhythms and hollow drums are transformed into symphonic microcosms, such songs as the masterpieces *Nicht Wiedersehen, Revelge, Der Tamboursg'sell* and, greatest of all, *Wo die schönen Trompeten blasen*. These are at the extreme in mood from the no less masterly expression of pastoral freshness in *Ich ging mit Lust durch einen grünen Wald*. Hearing the macabre relentlessness of *Der Tamboursg'sell*, in which the drummer-boy awaits execution, one ponders on the marvellous setting Mahler might have made of Kipling's poem 'Danny Deever'. Incidentally, the *Wunderhorn* songs are most effective when a selection of four or five is performed. They were not composed as an entity and to perform them together exposes too clearly the superiority to the remainder of three or four of them.

In each of the next three symphonies Mahler used a *Wunderhorn* song as an emotional climacteric. And in each he took an enormous step forward: he grew as man and artist from symphony to symphony, almost from song to song. Although in some ways the First Symphony is a better organized work than the Second, containing more 'advanced' music in the finale, the sheer audacity of the scale of the Second shows how Mahler's powers were growing. The *Wunderhorn* symphonies are a religious triptych, representing Mahler's search for a firm belief and for an answer to his questions about the mystery of existence.

The human voice is used in the Second, Third and Fourth Symphonies and Mahler provided a 'programme' for each of them, although he snatched it away again because he was hypersensitive about being dubbed a 'programmatic' instead of an 'absolute' composer, regarding himself as the antithesis of Richard Strauss. In 1897, when Symphony No. 2 was published, he wrote to Arthur Seidl: [1]

> You hit the nail on the head when you say that my music achieves a programme as the final explanation of feelings and ideas whereas Strauss's programme is the result of a planned quota. . . . When I draft a large-scale composition I invariably reach the point where I have to use the word as a carrier of my musical idea.

The programme of the Second Symphony is self-evident, even without Mahler's 'crutch', as is the use of Beethoven's Ninth Symphony as a musical model. The first movement is the funeral rite of the 'Titan' of the First Symphony; it asks: 'Why did you live, why suffer? Is it all nothing but a huge terrible joke?' [2] The second and third movements are nostalgia, happy and bitter; for the fourth movement a voice leads the soul to God and in the colossal finale there are the Day of Judgment, resurrection and love. Death and transfiguration, in other words.

Mahler's genius for creating a world of sound in which to convey the full force of his ideas, musical and moral, is at high pressure in the first movement.[3] That marvellous stormy opening (whether it derives from Berlioz or Wagner is irrelevant):

Ex. 8

---

[1] Alma Mahler, *Gustav Mahler, Briefe, 1879–1911* (Berlin, 1924).

[2] Letter to M. Marschalk, 26th March 1896.

[3] Sketched in 1888 and originally named *Totenfeier* ('Funeral Feast').

+bassoons and double bassoon

is fissionary material for a host of derivative themes, all centred on C minor, all funeral-march-like in character. The contrast comes with a harmonic change to E major and a simple, aspiring and beautiful melody that could only have been written by Mahler (and not only because of the *appoggiature*). This theme, first heard with a version of Ex. 8 as a counterpoint, is scored and used at each of its appearances with almost tentative restraint. If Mahler had been the composer his detractors believe that he was, one could imagine the lush treatment this tune would have received. It is, of course, the first hint of the 'Resurrection' theme of the finale:

Ex. 9

Mahler's scheme in this movement allows for an enlarged exposition and compressed development, each shedding different light on the material. Although he writes for a vast orchestra in this symphony (with six horns and six trumpets, increased to ten of each for the finale) his economy in its use is very marked. Mahler is, in fact, an economical composer except where inventiveness is concerned. What could be lovelier than the G minor introduction to the return of the slow theme in C major, when two oboes are accompanied by trumpets? Or more shattering than the famous dissonant chords containing every note of the C minor scale? The movement is one of Mahler's finest and best organized. His problem was how to follow it, knowing that he had planned the finale as the true climax of the symphony. He rejected, as he had in the First Symphony, the traditional symphonic *Adagio* and substituted—after specifying a five-minute pause—two short movements in complete contrast. His thoughts about this, expressed in a letter dated 25th March 1903 to Julius Buths (who was to conduct the symphony at the Lower Rhine Festival), are important and surprising:

According to you the main pause in the concert is to be between the fourth and fifth movements. I am amazed how you spotted instinctively the right and natural place in this work for a pause, in contrast to my own recommendation. I have long been of a like opinion and each performance I conduct has strengthened this view.

(It seems extraordinary that Mahler should have sanctioned a long pause between the *Urlicht* movement and the finale, the practice of playing them almost without a break now being standard.)

However, there should be a fairly lengthy breathing-space after the first movement because the second movement does not come out as an absolute contrast after the first when played immediately. This is my own fault. . . . I composed the *Andante* as a sort of intermezzo, like an echo from long past days in the life of him whom we accompanied to the grave in the first movement—days when all was sunshine and happiness. . . . This second movement stands on its own and in a certain sense interrupts the earnest and relentless course of events.

He was right. The *Andante moderato* is too great a contrast, enchanting though it is as a piece of music. A little too artfully contrived, though, in its sophisticated bucolicism, too consciously an orchestral showpiece in its elegant, relaxed delicacy, a nineteenth-century reflection of Haydn's Paris symphonies with a Tchaikovskyan *pizzicato* for good measure. Yet entrancing. The third movement too presents similar problems. This is an orchestral version of the *Wunderhorn* song about St Anthony preaching to the fishes, who, like mankind also, listen but do not mend their ways. The song and the text are ironic and satirical, but can music express satire and irony in purely instrumental sound? A few raucous woodwind squawks do not convey satire. So on that level this movement fails, I think, but succeeds (which is more important) as a brilliantly original *scherzo* with very potent suggestions of terror and disillusionment.

It is by the masterly cumulative tension of the coda of this *scherzo* that Mahler re-establishes his grip on his design. The two final movements can be regarded as one, the fourth being an integral prelude in D♭ to the fifth. The contralto sings the *Wunderhorn* song *Urlicht*, her voice unforgettably breaking the silence after the end of the preceding movement. A chorale for brass and woodwind emphasizes the solemnity of the mood, an example of Mahler in spellbinding vein. It seems and sounds so simple, so motionless, so timeless, yet there are twenty-one changes of time-signature in the first thirty-five bars and such inventive subtleties of orchestration as the use of two piccolos for a counterpoint to the vocal line, a delightfully ethereal effect.

The huge finale shows the young Mahler handling the most ambitious set-piece he had yet written with unerring confidence. The orchestral upheaval at the start, pointing the parallel with Beethoven's Ninth, gives way to a magnificent passage of scene-setting, unhurried, theatrical and portentous. Eclectic too, as there is little point in denying; not only are there reminiscences of Beethoven but of the Wagner of *Lohengrin* and, even more fruitfully and significantly, of the Verdi of *Aïda* (Act II) and *Otello* (the entry of Otello in Act IV). As usual Mahler weaves his fabric from a skein of thematic cross-references, anticipations and cross-fertilizations. Off-stage horn-calls and what can only be called fanfare-fantasias prepare for the violent percussive outburst which precedes a wild popular march. This passage has aroused scorn, even from avowed Mahlerians, but one of the features for which we cherish him is this ability to take basic elements of popular, even vulgar music, whether folk-pastoral or from the barracks tavern, and metamorphose them into symphonic material, as Beethoven did in the finale of the Ninth Symphony, as Puccini did in Act II of *La Bohème* and Vaughan Williams was to do in *A London Symphony*. Mahler saw this passage as a 'procession of rich and poor . . . a march of the dead to the Judgement'. It is like a Resurrection scene painted by Breughel (or, nearer to our day, by Stanley Spencer).

The last section of the finale, prefaced by a strange orchestral stillness, punctuated by distant fanfares and mysterious bird-calls—a forerunner of the similar passage in the *Abschied* of *Das Lied von der Erde*—culminates in the magical soft entry of the chorus singing Klopstock's hymn *Auferstehung* (Resurrection). Yet, to clinch his point, Mahler adds a verse of his own, given first to the contralto soloist: 'O glaube, mein Herz, O glaube'— 'O believe, my heart . . . thou wert not born in vain, hast not suffered in vain.' He is at his best setting his own words: one senses the joint inspiration. The tremendous peroration is an uplifting experience; hearing it, one receives a vicarious impression of what it must have been like to hear a great operatic finale controlled by Mahler from the conductor's desk. The end is in E♭ major, the key of the Eighth Symphony, with which this 'Resurrection' symphony is linked. Writing of this finale enthusiastically, I am nevertheless aware that it is not to all tastes and that many people find it pretentious and sanctimonious: Mahler, as one wit has said, wearing his ecclesiastical *Lederhosen*. Well, they are a good fit.

A Viennese critic after the first performance there of the Third Symphony in D minor wrote that its composer deserved a few years in gaol. Since then, by less hostile pens, it has been described as a formal disaster. I disagree. Not only do I think it shows an advance in musical power on the Second, but I think it is a better balanced artistic design, in spite of its six movements; and especially that the difficulties of the first movement have been much exaggerated (its duration too: 'nearly forty-five minutes', says one writer, who must have heard some odd performances. Thirty-five suffice).

Mahler, as stated earlier, had contemplated calling the symphony *Pan*, or even *The Joyful Science*, after Nietzsche's book *Die fröhliche Wissenschaft*. He planned seven movements, the last being a *Wunderhorn* setting, *Wir geniessen die himmlischen Freuden*, which later found its proper place as the finale of the Fourth Symphony. In its final version No. 3 has six movements: 1. Summer marches in. 2. What the flowers of the meadow tell me. 3. What the animals of the forest tell me. 4. What night tells me. 5. What the morning bells tell me. 6. What love tells me. These titles are pointers, no more: the symphony is an exultant celebration of life, physical and spiritual, sensuous and animal. While he was finishing it he described it to Anna von Mildenburg as 'of such magnitude that it mirrors the whole world—one is, so to speak, an instrument played on by the universe. . . . In my symphony the whole of nature finds a voice. . . . Passages in it seem so uncanny I can hardly recognize them as my work.' Schoenberg, as we have seen, heard the symphony as a battle between good and evil.

The gigantic first movement is better appreciated if the listener eschews analysis and concentrates instead on absorbing its atmosphere, its astonishing creation of a mood of protean

energy unleashed. Its impressive and portentous opening theme
for eight horns:

Ex. 10

symbolizes the force of nature but gives way at once to a long
mysterious prelude, another example of potent Mahlerian scene-
setting, with eerie brass *glissandi*, declamatory trumpet solos,
exhortatory trombones—all the fingerprints which the klepto-
maniac Mahler impresses on his score, pressing their emotional
connotations into his service and rendering them Mahlerian.
Twice, like some aural flashbacks to a vivid image retained from
childhood or youth, come extraordinary episodes of plebeian
brass music. A great conductor of this symphony, as Barbirolli
was, can convey the hallucinatory quality of these outbursts and
set them within the context of the surrounding music, so that the
movement sounds vast but also concise, its stormy coda the
inevitable conclusion to an immense drama.

It is Mahler's triumph in this symphony that the succeeding
shorter inner movements 'fit' the scheme more comfortably than
in the 'Resurrection'. The second movement, another in the
Blumine mould, is again highly sophisticated, even prettified,
far from elemental. But the kaleidoscopic effect of the orchestration is sufficient in itself for most ears; Mahler can scarcely be
blamed if his turns of phrase have become clichés for a later
generation because of the uses to which they were put by the
émigré musicians who, knowing their Mahler better than most at

the time, drew so heavily on him for Hollywood film scores in the 1930s and 1940s. The rustic start to the third movement, though it derives from the early *Wunderhorn* song *Ablösung im Sommer*, has an unmistakable affinity with the ballet music of *Aïda*. The level of inspiration drops, despite much ingenuity, until the trio, where the mood-painter's magic takes over for a wonderful evocative posthorn solo, the memory of … of what? A bugle in childhood, a horn sounding in the Salzkammergut? Youth's Magic Horn itself? It hardly matters. Its spacious, distant quality is as haunting as the natural trumpet solo in a similar atavistic passage in Vaughan Williams's *Pastoral Symphony*.

Although another riotous popular outburst occurs in the *scherzo* repeat, it is the posthorn that stays in the mind and prepares us for the Nietzsche setting in the fourth movement: 'O Mensch! Gib acht'—'O Man, take heed, what saith the midnight?', the same midnight song of Zarathustra which also inspired some of Delius's finest music in *A Mass of Life*. Mahler sets it for contralto, with one of his most profound and 'yearning' melodies as a counterpoint. It is one of Mahler's 'lost-to-the-world' movements, the words 'Gib acht' set to the descending F♯–E which opens the first theme of the first movement of the Ninth Symphony, both passages being in D major, and similar to the 'Ewig' phrase in the *Abschied* of *Das Lied von der Erde*. There is a wealth of musical and psychological interest to be derived from the cross-references, intentional or subconscious, between Mahler works—a game any listener can play; in this symphony there are several important cross-references between movements, notably the return of the climax of the first-movement exposition as the climax of the finale.

From the darkness of this sublime movement Mahler jerks us into the joyous light of another circle of the *Wunderhorn* paradise, where 'the quiring of the young-ey'd cherubins' (or, to be musically more accurate, of the *Otello ragazzi*) is heard— 'Bimm bamm'—and the bells chime for noonday joy, not midnight melancholy. (Britten, I suspect, was influenced by these sounds when he wrote *Noyes Fludde* and parts of the *War Requiem*.) The women's chorus sing 'Es sungen drei Engel' (Three angels sang a sweet song, the sound to heaven rises). The contralto sings the refrain which will recur in the finale of the Fourth Symphony in another context. Here it is the melody for St Peter's 'I have broken Thy commandments'; there for the angels who bake the bread, but, more significantly, for St Peter in heaven.

In the Second Symphony Mahler's grand design was to work to a climacteric in the finale. A finale on that scale in No. 3 would have been ridiculously out of mood, but a substantial clinching movement was needed. He gives us his first full-scale symphonic *Adagio*, the nearest he was to go to a Brucknerian fullness of harmony and spiritual calm (was it, perhaps, designed as a tribute to his old friend and encourager?). To Anna von Mildenburg he confided:

The motto to this movement is 'Father, see these wounds of mine! Let not be lost one creature of thine.' I could almost call the movement 'What God tells me'. And truly, in the sense that God can only be understood as love. And so my work . . . begins with inanimate nature and ascends to the love of God.

The *adagios* of Beethoven and of Elgar come to mind as one listens to this movement, in which the two melodies on which it is based are subjected, with infinite resource, to Mahler's doctrine of continuous development and variation—real 'unending melody'. Yet there is a crisis—Mahler cannot leave the world behind, however hard he may try; the dissonance in the central section is a forceful reminder to listeners today that Mahler was little more than a decade away from the Ninth and Tenth Symphonies. In the coda D major is reached in an apotheosis which is perhaps too rhetorically overblown, too extended, to carry conviction. Yet when one has said that, the overwhelming impression is of a masterpiece—one that seems to grow shorter and simpler the more one hears it. For all its size and scale, it is an intimate work.

The Fourth Symphony in G major of 1899–1900 can be regarded as an epilogue to the first three symphonies. It is Mahler's most intimate, small-scaled symphony, with a reduced orchestra and hardly any grandiose effects. One cannot speak of naïveté in connection with such a subtle and disciplined composition, but its mood is certainly childlike in the most felicitous way. No wonder it is Mahler's most popular and approachable symphony, and it is the first in which he kept to the four movements of the classical pattern. He thought of subtitling it *Humoresque*—a clue (if any were needed) to its links with the *Wunderhorn* songs and especially with *Wir geniessen die himmlischen Freuden*, composed in March 1892. An early 'blueprint' for the symphony shows that its conception preceded the Second and Third—still further proof that Mahler's symphonies are a continuous interlinked chain, or, to use a literary parallel, a vast autobiographical novel, of which each symphony is a chapter. Paul Bekker's theory, disparaged by Neville Cardus, that the whole symphony was germinated by this song seems to me to be convincing. Each movement is thematically interconnected, in Mahler's usual allusively subtle way. In any case, here are Mahler's words to Natalie Bauer-Lechner in 1901: 'I really wanted to write a symphonic humoresque and it turned itself into a full symphony, whilst earlier when I wanted it to become a symphony it became the length of three—my Second and Third.'

The first movement is melodically profuse, its texture and structure an advance on anything Mahler had hitherto composed, the counterpoint never more inventive, the lucidity and freshness of the material often recalling Haydn rather than Schubert. Mahler's mood here is relaxed, the world's slings and arrows ignored if not forgotten. Not only is the delightful *insouciance* of the jingling opening unforgettable—he called it 'a divinely gay and deeply melancholical tune'—but there is the piercing beauty of this flute vision of paradise:

Ex. 11

which is to play so important a part.

Of such a well-known and well-loved work it is hardly necessary to do more than to give a reminder of its beauties: the exquisite coda of the first movement, for example—*sancta simplicitas* if ever one heard it; and the mildly spooky *scherzo*, so marvellously likened by Cardus to the shadows cast by candlelight on a nursery wall. In this fantasy-*Ländler* Mahler makes much use of a solo violin with a *scordatura* tuning of the strings, so that it plays a whole tone higher than the rest, to sound like 'ein Fiedel', a medieval forerunner of the violin and the origin of the word 'fiddle'. In an early sketch Mahler wrote of this passage 'Freund Hain spielt auf'. The friend Hain who plays was a ghostly fiddler leading the way to eternity or perdition. Mahler's devils and demons are off duty in this symphony and friend Hain is picturesque rather than macabre. However, one must recall Mahler's description of composing this symphony: [4]

Because of the compelling logic of a piece which I had to alter, all the following work turned topsy-turvy on me and to my astonishment it became plain to me I had entered a totally different realm, just as in a

[4] Letter to Bauer-Lechner, 25th July 1900.

dream one imagines oneself wandering through the flower-scented garden of Elysium and it suddenly changes to a nightmare of finding oneself in a Hades full of terrors. The spoors and emanations of these, to me, horrifying, mysterious worlds are often found in my compositions. This time it is a forest with all its mysteries and its horrors which forces my hand and weaves itself into my work. It becomes ever clearer to me that one does not compose, but is being composed.

Hence the chill that often grips this sunny work, even in the *Adagio*.

The end of the *scherzo*, after a subtle thematic allusion to the theme of the finale,

Ex. 12   Scherzo

Ex. 13   Finale

has a touch of astringency which vanishes in the *Adagio*, Mahler's most untroubled movement, although its serene flow is interrupted first by dancing and later by a passionate 'disintegrating', as powerful as anything in the Fifth and Sixth Symphonies and obviously the 'Hades of terrors' mentioned above. In a superb passage near the end Ex. 11 bursts upon the listener like a religious fresco of Paradise. Mahler used variation form in this movement, and was thus able with uncanny skill to sustain moods of childlike bliss and adult devotion side by side and interlinked. It is the perfect prelude to the song-finale, in which the soprano, who must sound unaffectedly simple with no trace of archness, sings of the child's vision of heaven, 'cloudless blue sky' with Martha baking the bread and angelic voices hymning St Cecilia. The scoring is delicate, the key is a radiant consoling E major.

The G major symphony was published in 1902 but Mahler revised it several times. It is hard to believe that so enchanting a work should have had so cool an initial reception—even Alma disliked it at first—and that Mahler described it as a 'persecuted stepchild'. His final revision, for his two New York performances, was on 11th October 1910, but Erwin Stein in the 1920s discovered a set of proofs with still further extensive revisions aimed, as usual, at extra clarity.[5] These include changes of dynamics and expression marks and such alterations in the scoring as the reinforcement of the oboe melody at four bars after fig. 7 in the slow movement by muted trumpet, cor anglais and horn, and a thinning out of the accompaniment in the finale. Various *tempo* directions are also changed. It is as if, every time he conducted his own works, he recomposed them.

[5] See 'The Unknown Last Version of Mahler's Fourth Symphony' in *Orpheus in New Guises* (London, 1953), pp. 31–3.

12　Rückert Symphonies

When discussing the three central instrumental symphonies, Nos. 5, 6 and 7, several writers seem to have been so dazzled by their complexity and ingenuity that it is difficult, when listening to the music, to equate it with the verbal contortions and metaphors employed. There is perhaps a parallel with the late quartets of Beethoven, which for years were regarded as on such a high plane of musical philosophy that hardly a coherent paragraph could be written about them. Bernard Shaw was not merely an iconoclast but a heretic when he wrote in 1894 of the late quartets as 'beautiful, simple, straightforward, unpretentious, perfectly intelligible'. Mahler's three middle symphonies are not simple and straightforward, but they are beautiful and intelligible. Few composers have benefited more from the invention of the long-playing record and tape-recording. Only in the second half of the twentieth century has it been possible fully to absorb these works, not through the score and the memories of isolated performances but by constant study of their sound in a series of superb interpretations. Far from breeding contempt, familiarity increases admiration for their mastery. They are complex, but Mahler's grand designs are logical and purposive, becoming clearer and simpler with each repetition.

Mahler was sensitive to the taunt of 'programme music', and there is perhaps an element of determination to be 'absolute' about these instrumental works. But they mark an intensification of his processes of musical thought, and, for all their size and elaborate orchestration, a further refinement of the means of expression. Together they form one vast symphony and, as always, there are thematic allusions and cross-references. The *Wunderhorn* is still an influence, but the germinating songs for these three symphonies are the setting of poems by Friedrich Rückert (1788–1866) which Mahler began at Maiernigg in 1901. These songs were conceived with an orchestral accompaniment of refined, subtle and almost sparse texture, an extension of the clarity everywhere found in the Fourth Symphony and which he outlined in 1899 to Natalie Bauer-Lechner:

Formerly I liked to decorate my compositions with unusual details and to make their external form completely unconventional, just as a young man delights in conspicuous clothes. In later life he's glad to be average and to appear inconspicuously so long as what is inside him sets him apart from others. That's why today I'm satisfied when I can pour music into the usual moulds, and I avoid all innovations unless they are absolutely necessary.

Not to be taken wholly at face value, of course, but certainly a confession of a change of tactics.

Mahler composed four Rückert songs in 1901 and began the Fifth Symphony. He set the first three of what was to become the cycle *Kindertotenlieder* (*Songs about the death of children*). At the time he was unmarried and had not met Alma: what moved him in these poems was that one of the two children whom Rückert had lost was named Ernst, the name of Mahler's beloved younger brother who had died in 1874. This boy's death was the most searing experience of Mahler's childhood and one can easily perceive that he would wish, as a mature artist, to commemorate him. One might imagine such a thing had never been done before when one reads such accusations as 'self-tormenting exhibitionism' (Redlich) made against Mahler, many of them no doubt deriving from Alma's superstitions about the songs' application to their own children—superstitions which I suspect did not occur to her until she wrote her book some

years after Mahler's death. He completed the cycle with two more
songs composed in 1904. It is his greatest song-cycle. Though
sombre in mood as befits the subject, there is no trace of sentimentality nor of morbid introspection. If this was a conscious
attempt to exorcize a ghost, it must have proved successful
because tragedy is transcended and the music attains a mood of
serene acceptance. Moreover, there is surely a deliberate sym-
bolism in the poems Mahler chose (five out of a total of 428): in
the first the rising sun, 'the light that gladdens all the world';
in the second, brightness returning 'to the source of all light';
the vision in the fourth song of sunlight on the hills; and, finally,
God's hand protecting the children from the storm. A compassionate, affirmatory approach, matched by music of tender-
ness and insight, scored with infallible mastery. The first, *Nun
will die Sonn' so hell aufgeh'n*, is perhaps the most wonderful,
but the second, *Nun seh' ich wohl*, anticipates the lyrical line of
Das Lied von der Erde. The cor anglais and *pizzicato* in the third
song suggest Bach, and the last two songs make a perfect contrast, the fourth being visionary and the fifth dramatic, with its
representation of the storm (so economically yet graphically
depicted) and ending with the consoling lullaby—note the horn
solo—which gives another 'child's view of heaven' and is an
outstanding example of Mahler's ability to convey poignancy as
effectively in the major mode as in the minor. The greatness of
the music lies in the fusion of the sinuous melodic vocal line
with an orchestral support in which every instrumental inflec-
tion is a counterpoint. Although there are no thematic links
between the songs, the impression of organic unity is strong, so
powerfully unifying is the mood of the cycle.

The five other Rückert settings, all composed in 1901–2, are
beautiful individually but have no binding emotional theme.
They too are notable for subtle refinement of scoring, a pointer
to Mahler's progress towards the marvels of the introduction to
Part II of the Eighth Symphony and to the almost vocal elo-

quence of the instrumental writing in *Das Lied von der Erde*. The delicacy of *Ich atmet' einen linden Duft* and of *Blicke mir nicht* are no distance from the Chinese porcelain of the inner movements of *Das Lied*. The best known of Mahler's songs, *Ich bin der Welt abhanden gekommen*, has become an epitome of his spiritual withdrawal—though in fact no man was more engaged with life at all levels, an active not a passive artist—but it illustrates the deep satisfaction he found in his annual retreat from the hurly-burly of opera to the inner hurly-burly of composing. Such a beautiful melody it is, expressive of the escapist in us all. The countryside, love, poetry, music—would we not abandon ourselves to them if only. . . . This idealistic personal yearning Mahler embodied in this great song, but its wider universal significance was to be expressed in the *Abschied* of *Das Lied von der Erde* in similar but even more subtle melodic curves. The most remarkable song of the five is *Um Mitternacht* (At Midnight), scored for woodwind and brass, with timpani and harp. In the friendless midnight the poet gives his power into the hands of God. Mahler's precise delineation of tone-colour calls here for an oboe d'amore to convey the lonely melancholy of Rückert's mood:

The song has the solemnity of a chorale, but the note of passionate individual entreaty is strong. Whereas *Ich bin der Welt* represents Mahler the spiritual hedonist, *Um Mitternacht* shows us the religious ascetic.

Symphonies 5, 6 and 7 may be designated the most 'Viennese' of Mahler's works, with Symphonies 2, 3 and 4 the most 'Austrian' and Nos. 9 and 10 the most cosmopolitan. The Fifth is

Mahler's 'Eroica', progressing from tragedy to triumph. Although it is designated as in C♯ minor, the symphony 'feels' to be in D major. It begins in C♯ minor and moves through A minor, D major and F major to end in D—these tonal centres combine to give a major seventh with D in root position. This chord provides the symphony with overall tension. The symphony's form is also misleading. Although there are five movements, the symphony is in three parts. Part I comprises the opening funeral march and its thematically related stormy sequel; Part II is the *Scherzo*; and Part III consists of two linked movements, the *Adagietto* and Rondo-Finale.

The opening trumpet-call, derived from the first movement of the Fourth Symphony, is followed by a funeral march, obviously related to the 1901 *Wunderhorn* song *Der Tamboursg'sell*. Being a symphonic march, it is given two trios, the first a wild and intensely contrapuntal section in B♭ minor, which is followed by a recapitulation of the march ending with a direct quotation from the first of the *Kindertotenlieder*, its last line 'Heil sei dem Freudenlicht der Welt!' (I bless the light that gladdens all the world). This is a signal for the second trio (A minor), quieter in mood and given to the strings. It is thematically related to a brass motif in the first trio but utterly transformed (see Ex. 15 opposite).

Binding each section together is the trumpet-call, sometimes strident, sometimes bodeful and, at the end, muted and echoed by a flute. The second movement is marked 'with the utmost vehemence' and develops the B♭ minor section of the march as a Tchaikovskyan battleground on which Mahler can fight his demons. It is savage, exhilarating music, a classic passage of Mahlerian ability to extract the maximum emotional and contrapuntal effect from fairly commonplace material. But it is not all storm. Cellos and clarinets are given a consoling theme, later heard with poetic effect on the horns. The climax is a chorale in D major, majestically intoned, but it is not allowed at this stage

Ex. 15

to emerge triumphantly and the movement ends with a mysterious coda, all half-lights and fantasies.

The central *Scherzo* is on a large scale, which has deluded some commentators into an excessively ponderous view of it.

Mahler, after its first performance, wrote of 'dancing stars' in connection with this movement, which is mainly cheerful and gay—and rather Lehárish. The gently lilting second section for strings is the stuff of operetta, but the movement is dominated by the *concertante* part for solo horn. Some of this is boisterous, but Mahler's understanding of the instrument's romantic capability is at its most acute in the Trio section where the colours and moods of twilight descend over the orchestra and the horn calls poignantly while the strings suggest a Sibelian lake across which the echoes come. The whole passage, with its marvellous use of *pizzicato*, is intensely atmospheric, suggesting some legend or folk-memory in Mahler's subconscious mind. It lasts too long for the good of the proportions of the movement, but the return to the hectic world of the *scherzo* is managed in a manner worthy of Schubert:

Ex. 16

The joyous recapitulation of the waltz cannot banish the poetic memory, and before the coda the horn's evocation of faery lands forlorn is heard again—and again during the coda.

Part III begins with the famous *Adagietto* for harp and strings which used to be wrenched from its context and played separately. (This was fair enough when it was the only way of introducing Mahler's name into an orchestra's repertory, but the practice must now be abhorred.) Its relationship to the Rückert song *Ich bin der Welt* is obvious, though it is always an instrumental symphonic movement, never a symphonic song, its middle section expressing an unfulfilled yearning of special poignancy. We are roused from its lulling reverie by a gentle horn-call; the bassoon quotes a phrase from the *Wunderhorn* song, *Lob des hohen Verstandes*, about the song-contest between the cuckoo and the nightingale judged by the donkey. Thus Mahler serves notice that he is about to give a display of academic prowess, fugue and all. It is a brilliant display for most of its course, the main theme assembled from the fragments hinted at the start, each theme emerging effortlessly from its predecessor, the *Adagietto* theme transformed into a kind of march.

There is nothing neurotic in this exuberant exhibition of Mahler's mastery. Only towards the end does he falter while 'filling in' rather repetitively before his final climax—the return of the chorale from the second movement. This is perhaps rather contrived and is certainly too long signalled, but it is a hard heart which cannot rejoice in the life-giving zest of this astonishing movement, in itself proof that Mahler had a sense of fun.

With Symphony No. 6 in A minor Mahler took another protean step in his development as a musician. It is a tragic work, but it is tragedy on a high plane, classical in conception and execution. To describe this music in the jargon of the psychoanalyst's couch, in terms of neuroses and complexes, is to traduce its finely tempered steely spirit. For while it is of the utmost sensitivity and responsiveness, it is also the music of a valiant and noble-hearted man, grappling with fears, doubts and the

117

fates but remaining resolute, even in defeat. Serious though it is, it is not unrelievedly gloomy. Mahler knew the need for constant contrast: 'Change and conflict are the secret of effective music.' [1] In all his works he lays immense responsibilities and burdens on the conductor but never more than in the last five symphonies. Not only must the 'architecture' of each work be comprehensively grasped, but there must be acute appreciation of the need for continuously fluctuating variations of tempo.

Mahler himself found No. 6 difficult to conduct and correctly prophesied that its day would dawn only when conductors, orchestras and audiences were familiar with all his work. For years it was rarely performed—the United States did not hear it until Mitropoulos conducted it in New York in 1947—but this unhappy state of affairs no longer obtains and now it is clear that this is probably (I would say certainly) Mahler's greatest symphony, taken as a whole. He revised it several times, even switching the original order (*Scherzo, Andante*) of the two middle movements but then changing his mind. There are arguments for both ways, depending on whether tonality or emotional logic affects the listener more strongly. Mahler, as we have seen, was deeply affected by the work and later, from superstition, deleted the third of the three 'blows of fate' from the finale. Some conductors restore it.

Notwithstanding the length (eighty-one minutes) of this work and the very large orchestra used, the symphonic argument is comparatively taut and unified. Once again Mahler's favourite interval of a fourth is exploited to its full capacity, but the principal organic feature of the thematic material is the tragedy motif, the major-minor chord, heard in the first instance as a loud common chord fading away while the major third is turned into the minor:

---

[1] Letter to Marschalk, 26th April 1896.

The rhythm in the accompaniment, marked *a*, pervades the symphony.

Much depends on the interpretation of the very first bars. Not summer this time, but 'modern music' marches in with this sinister, tramping start. It is marked *Allegro energico, ma non troppo,* and this is reinforced by a further instruction in German: *Heftig, aber markig* (vehement, but plenty of vigour). If, as often (alas) happens, only the *energico* and *heftig* are observed, without their qualifying speed limit, disaster inevitably follows and the movement, instead of being tragic, becomes merely strident and aggressive. True, vehemence and fury are there, but if they are allowed to become unbridled ferocity the point of the work is lost. Those who regard Mahler as an undisciplined composer might profitably study the design of this first movement—not excessively long at just over twenty minutes—and note especially the restraint with which he treats his F major second subject (said by Alma to depict her)—a consoling but by no means over-romanticized contrast with the opening march, although it has already been foreshadowed in the first-subject group:

The interested listener may detect a *Heldenleben*-like sound in the richness of some of the scoring. Ironically, for Mahler referred

119

to himself as an 'old-fashioned' composer, it was the 'boldness
of harmony' in this symphony which Schoenberg admired.
Alban Berg was equally impressed, describing it to Webern as
'the *only* Sixth, despite the *Pastoral*'—a meaningless but well-
meant tribute. Perhaps he was thinking of three remarkably
imaginative episodes in this movement: one in which the sleigh-
bells of the Fourth Symphony seem to be purposely distorted;
the second in which Mahler evokes the sound of cow-bells
heard from afar when one is high in the Alps, a passage of unforgettable poetry, unearthly, the cow-bells strangely like some
electronic pastoral ghost-noise; and the third an equally strange
evocation, this time with the celesta making its symphonic début,
suggesting eighteenth-century echoes amid the twentieth-
century *Sturm und Drang*. The cow-bells, Mahler explained,
'are the last earthly sounds heard from the valley far below by the
departing spirit on the mountain top'. Clearly, too, their sound
vividly recalled his youth. When he was nineteen he described
to his friend Steiner 'shadowy memories of my life, passing
before me like long-forgotten ghosts'. Among these he specified
a meadow 'where the cow-bells lull me to dreaming' and of
hearing 'the evening bells in the village below'.

The *Scherzo* also opens with a strong tramping rhythm, but
it is a fatal interpretative mistake to fail to differentiate between
the *tempi* of the first movement and this *scherzo*. It is a remarkable and elusive movement. In fifteen lines about it that fine
scholar Hans Redlich,[2] after describing it as a 'sinister Hoff-
mannèsque puppet-show' (because of the xylophone), uses the
adjectives 'spookish', 'ghostly', 'diabolical', 'exotic', 'cata-
strophic', 'grim', 'fiery', 'lurid' and 'demoniacal'. Mahler, it
seems to me, accomplished his purpose with more subtlety.'
Might it not be that the personal experiences of Hans Redlich
and his like, their enforced exile from Germany or Austria

[2] H. F. Redlich, *Bruckner and Mahler* (London, 1963), p. 207.

through the scourge of Nazism, distorted their responses to certain aspects of Mahler's music, lending it a specific personal association which—understandably enough—overlaid its substance with an almost hysterical intensity? Each listener, of course, may interpret the music to his own fancy. There are underlying sardonic humour, brief hints of the horn passage from the *Scherzo* of No. 5, and some delicate pastiche Haydn of uncloying charm which prepares the way for the *altväterisch* (in the style of a bygone age) trio, with its elegant oboe. The movement ends with an enigmatic passage—beating drum, flutes, violin solo—thoroughly in keeping with the tragic mood of the symphony.

For the main theme of the *Andante moderato* in E♭ major Mahler refers to one of the *Kindertotenlieder*, but the movement is mellow, relaxed and even idyllic, in the form of a slow rondo. The cow-bells are heard again, the horn calls romantically. Restraint is once more the keynote, but the beauty of the music may easily cause us to overlook (as, indeed, it should) the technical skill, notably the novel and subtle merging, or overlapping, of themes (as in the minuet of Symphony No. 3 and in the first movement of No. 4, where the development section and recapitulation are so intricately and effectively interlinked). Placed third, this *Andante* makes a poignant prelude to the crushing power of the immense finale. Mahler here seems to challenge his superb mastery of large-scale structures and wins triumphantly. All that has gone before is but the preface to this clinching essay in tragedy, opening in C minor with a tense and mysterious introduction containing the principal material—swirling harp *glissandi*, a soaring violin theme (note the rhythm *a* from Ex. 17):

Ex. 19

the tragedy-motif, a baying tuba whose theme is also flavoured by the pervasive rhythm *a* and is based on the ascending octave of Ex. 19. Among further themes is a sombre woodwind chorale.

A march tune, still in C minor, leads into the A minor *Allegro energico*, invigorating and strident. Twice the cow-bells return, enclosing a savage march. Three times the *Allegro energico* is interrupted by the return of the introduction. After the first interruption it resumes with two development sections. At the height of each, a hammer-blow is heard followed by the tragedy-motif roared by trombones, with unison trumpets as background. After the second return of the introduction the *Allegro* reaches an exultant climax but the tragedy-motif halts it. This is where the third hammer-blow occurs. Those who expect a melodramatic metallic crash for these blows, as Richard Strauss did, are disappointed; Mahler specified a non-metallic thud, 'like an axe-stroke', of the bass drum. The excitement of the movement is cumulative and intensified by moments of lyrical expansiveness. Despite its thirty-two minutes, it is so packed with incident that it seems almost compressed. In the coda there is a lofty Brucknerian chorale for the horns, as though the malignancy of Fate had been quelled. But, like Thomas Hardy, Mahler the fatalist—for such he was, rather than a pessimist— believed that someone was waiting round the corner to club him down, and this mighty work ends in its original key with the tragedy-motif as a *fortissimo* minor triad, subsiding into the sullen silence of defeat.

In the Sixth Symphony, and especially in its finale, Mahler's individual use of symphonic form reached its highest peak so far. The sonorities are still new-sounding and fascinating, the counterpoint supreme; his constant variation of his themes is masterly—the 'Alma' theme, for example, always slightly different, always elusive; but the sonorities and the substance seem to have been simultaneously created, so inseparable are they. Much may therefore be expected from Symphony No. 7

in B minor, for we have seen how Mahler developed with each successive work—shed a skin, in Cardus's graphic phrase. Yet even though Mahler's symphonies are now as much appreciated as they were formerly derided, the Seventh has remained the least understood and accepted of the ten; even long-serving champions in his cause have called it a failure, or 'cranky', or repetitive (because its design is so similar to that of No. 5). Few conductors can bring this work off as effectively as they can No. 5, or even No. 9. Does this mean that the fault lies in the music itself? I do not think so. It is a complex, extravagant, highly sophisticated, mercurial symphony beside which No. 6 is comparatively straightforward. It needs exceptionally close understanding and co-operation between conductor and orchestra if it is to make its proper effect, not to mention thorough rehearsal. In none of Mahler's symphonies is it more essential for a modern orchestra's string sections to be taught the correct and subtle use of *portamento*. Much is made of Mahler's admission that the second and fourth movements were composed in 1904 and the three others added a year later, a lack of unity being adduced. This criticism must be respected; one can refute it only by saying that 'unity' in a symphony is partly sensed as an emotional inevitability. (Binding movements together thematically is not an infallible passport to unity.) I sense this unity in the Seventh, and am convinced that Mahler's grand design succeeds.

Its subtitle could be 'the Romantic' or 'Nocturnes', for this is music 'about' night and dreams and, eventually, the return of day. It is Mahler's most glamorous symphony and it is a vast canvas, nearly eighty-seven minutes in length, the first movement lasting over twenty-three minutes. It is scored for a large orchestra (2 piccolos, 4 flutes, 3 oboes, cor anglais, E♭ clarinet, 3 clarinets in A, bass clarinet, 3 bassoons, contra-bassoon, tenor horn in B♭, 4 horns, 3 trumpets, 3 trombones, tuba, 2 harps, mandoline, guitar, much percussion, and strings). Yet the texture

Mahler

is translucent. Clarity, always clarity, every detail telling. In orchestration alone, this work is spellbinding. 'With me,' he boasted, 'all the instruments sing, even the brass and the kettle-drums.' There are prophetic features in the harmony, such as the superimposed fourths in the first movement, and the work appealed strongly on its first appearance to the new generation—to Hermann Scherchen, for instance, who was a viola-player before he became a conductor and was eighteen when No. 7 was first performed. He described it as 'my first whiff of a new artistic feeling, one that marked the transition to expressionism'. Schoenberg was impressed by its massive flexibility and poise. Writing to Mahler on 29th December 1909 he mentioned

perfect repose based on artistic harmony; something that set me in motion without simply upsetting my centre of gravity and leaving me to my fate; that drew me calmly and pleasingly into its orbit ... in a manner so measured and preordained that there are never any sudden jolts. ... I felt so many subtleties of form.

He had penetrated to the secret of this astonishing symphony: that Mahler's grip on the Haydn-Beethoven-Mozart sonata-form tradition was so strong and his own individuality so potent that an extraordinary impression of novelty and experiment is given within a classical structure on which a copious imagination has been given full play. The key structure of the symphony is B minor, followed by an E minor *Allegro con fuoco* which ends in E major; C minor for the second movement, D minor for the third, F major for the fourth and C major for the fifth.

The slow introduction to the first movement is dramatic and deliberate, the magnificent and pregnant first theme being allotted to the tenor horn. ('Here Nature roars', said Mahler.) As in the first movement of No. 4, the mosaic effect of the treatment of the material shows the cunningly experienced hand of an ultra-sophisticated musician. The intensely Romantic and 'Mahlerian' second subject, in C major, is a strong clue to the pervading mood of the work; it is juxtaposed with a typical march-like rhythm (similar to a comparable passage in No. 6). Part of the expressionism which attracted Scherchen is to be found in the trumpet-calls, the hushed strings, the anticipation of Bartók's night-music. With what mastery the movement is built to an ecstatic climax—a blaze of light in the darkness which returns, even more doom-laden and mysterious, before the aggressive coda.

The first of the two 'night-music' movements seems to recapture, in twentieth-century terms, the moonlit Romanticism of Mozart's *Don Giovanni* and *Marriage of Figaro*—perhaps the Spanish rhythm has a relevance to Seville. The echoing horns and woodwind, the *pizzicato* strings and the marvellous assortment of sounds—particularly the A♭ theme for the cellos—seem to constitute a determined re-creation of the elegance of eighteenth-century manners. Cow-bells are used, but how differently from No. 6. There they drifted to the ear impressionistically, the very sound of solitude; here they are near and mundane.

Mahler's direction for the central *scherzo* is 'Fluently, but not brisk (shadowy)'. For some commentators this haunting movement has a 'whiff of death'; others find it horrific and bitter, expressing cynicism and sarcasm. I am sceptical of the ability of instrumental music to be sarcastic, and while in no way wishing to deny the mysterious atmosphere of this movement, I align myself with Erwin Stein's poetic description: 'It is a child's fear of the dark that Mahler so compassionately describes.' That can be horrific enough, of course, and this *scherzo* marvellously depicts flickering firelight and grotesque shadows, with the gentle trio a calming lullaby. Waltz, *Ländler* and march are parodied during this satirical essay.

But night is for love too, and just as the Fifth had its *Adagietto* at this point, the Seventh has its *Andante amoroso*—a tender and romantic serenade, with swooning harmonies, the sound of the mandoline for wooing and a lyrical cello theme (the trio) for

design (repeated exposition in the first movement). All this is sufficient refutation of the old gibe that Mahler was an undisciplined sentimentalist. The severe classical training of his youth and his genius as a conductor of Beethoven and Mozart are the keystones of the Sixth Symphony. It is also a demonstration that his conducting was an integral part of his composing.

Yet there is an extra poignancy when we contemplate these masterpieces. They were composed when Mahler's music was not merely misunderstood by the critics but attacked with such vehemence that even he was thrown off balance and lost faith in his work. His anxieties when he conducted the first performances were more than first-night nerves. He made himself ill with revisions of the orchestral parts, constantly worrying over them. Schoenberg's words, published in an essay on Mahler in *Der Merker*, should be recalled:

How will they seek to answer for this: that Mahler had to say 'It seems I have been in error'? How will they seek to justify themselves when they are accused of having brought one of the greatest composers of all time to the point where he was deprived of the sole, the highest recompense for a creative mind, the recompense found when the artist's faith in himself allows him to say: 'I have *not* been in error'?

13 The Eighth Symphony

The Eighth Symphony is a throwback to the Mahler of Symphonies 2, 3 and 4 and a return to words as the carriers of his ideas. It is as if, after the secular, worldly confessions of Nos. 5, 6 and 7, he had returned to the search for redemption which had obsessed him in the 1890s. Alma is reported to have said, in a moment of exasperation, that 'Gustav is always on the telephone to God'. In No. 8 he was on the hot line. I have already quoted his description of how 'the *Spiritus Creator* took hold of me and shook me and drove me on' when he went to Maiernigg in 1906. He composed the symphony between 21st June and 18th August, and he told Schoenberg it was 'as if it had been dictated to me'—again the sense of 'being composed'. That it represents a profound spiritual experience cannot be gainsaid.

The intellectual plan of the symphony is characteristic of Mahler: to affirm the Christian faith and belief in the power of the Spirit as expressed in the ancient hymn *Veni, Creator Spiritus*, and to link this with Goethe's symbolic vision, in the closing scene of *Faust*, Part II, of the redemption of mankind through love as represented by the Eternal-Feminine (*Das Ewig-Weibliche*). In this scene Faust's soul is borne aloft by angels and granted salvation by the Virgin Mary (Mater Gloriosa). Mahler allots only two lines to the Virgin, but they are the key to the affinity he found between Goethe and Hrabanus Maurus, the ninth-century Archbishop of Mainz who is supposed to have written the hymn:

Komm! hebe dich zu höhern Sphären!
Wenn er dich ahnet, folgt er nach.

(Come then! rise to higher spheres!
Divining you, he will follow.)

And from the hymn:

Accende lumen sensibus,
Infunde amorem cordibus.

(Illuminate our senses,
Pour love into our hearts.)

There was a further association in Mahler's mind with what, in a letter to Alma written in June 1910 while he was rehearsing the symphony in Munich, he called 'the misunderstood "Platonic love"'. He continued:

The essence of it is really Goethe's idea that all love is generative, creative, and that there is a physical and spiritual generation which is the emanation of this 'Eros'. You have it in the last scene of *Faust*, presented symbolically . . . The wonderful discussion between Diotima and Socrates . . . gives the core of Plato's thought, his whole outlook on the world. . . . The comparison between [Socrates] and Christ is obvious and has arisen spontaneously in all ages. . . . In each case Eros as Creator of the world.

It may be helpful here to recall some of Diotima's discourse on love in Plato's *Symposium*, as translated by Shelley:

'Love, then, O Socrates, is not as you imagine the love of the beautiful.'—'What, then?'—'Of generation and production in the beautiful.'—'Why then of generation?'—'Generation is something eternal and immortal in immortality. It necessarily, from what has been confessed, follows that we must desire immortality together with what is good, since Love is the desire that good be for ever present to us. Of necessity Love must also be the desire of immortality.'

Now Mahler again, writing to Alma in June 1909 about the Goethe scene:

That which draws us by its mystic force, what every created thing, perhaps even the very stones, feels with absolute certainty as the centre of its being, what Goethe here—again employing an image—calls the eternal feminine—that is to say, the resting-place, the goal, in opposition to the striving and struggling towards the goal (the eternal masculine)—you are quite right in calling the force of love. Goethe ... expresses it with a growing clearness and certainty right on to the Mater Gloriosa—the personification of the eternal feminine!

Could there be more eloquent testimony to the extraordinary breadth of Mahler's human sympathy and to the power of the mysticism which impelled his creative activity, a mysticism with roots far deeper than the Catholicism superficially implicit in some of Goethe's text and deeper too than any atavistic Judaism? Indeed Mahler is an exemplar of Bryan Magee's assertion, in his splendid *Aspects of Wagner* (London, 1968), that 'it is only Jews who have escaped from their religious and intellectual tradition who have achieved greatness'.

So much for the impulse behind the Eighth Symphony. What of the music? It was the first completely choral symphony to be written—Vaughan Williams's *Sea Symphony* was not finished until 1908–9—and it justifies the title of symphony first by being indubitably symphonic in conception and secondly by its adaptation of sonata form in Part I. Some eminent commentators descry slow movement, *scherzo* and finale in Part II, but I think this involves 'bending' the music to fit the theory. Because of the vast forces involved, the work has become known as the 'Symphony of a Thousand', a description to be deplored because it encourages the view of No. 8 as a 'Barnum and Bailey' show, whereas Mahler's use of an exceptionally large orchestra was obviously not for grandiose effect but to ensure that balance between chorus and orchestra was as near perfect as possible. The scoring is for piccolo, 4 flutes, 4 oboes, cor anglais, 3 clarinets, E♭ clarinet, bass clarinet, 4 bassoons, contra-bassoon, 8 horns, 4 trumpets, 4 trombones, bass tuba, 3 timpani, bass drum, cymbals, gong, triangle, bells, glockenspiel, celesta, pianoforte, harmonium, organ, 2 harps, mandoline, strings, double chorus, boys' choir and eight soloists (three sopranos, two contraltos, tenor, baritone and bass). This was lampooned in the German press in 1911, just as the scoring of the Sixth Symphony had occasioned a cartoon of Mahler in 1906 captioned: 'My God, I've forgotten the motorhorn. Now I shall have to write another symphony.' Yet the predominant impression of No. 8 is not of torrents of sound but of the contrasts of subtle tone-colours and the luminous quality of the scoring. Rarely had Mahler shown such mastery of the large forces he required, rarely scored with such certainty. Unusually for him, there were few revisions and the score was ready for publication in 1907, though not published until 1911. Repeated hearings, such as the gramophone affords, reveal the remarkable thematic unity of the two movements: the work seems to grow shorter. In fact it is far from being the longest of his symphonies. At roughly seventy-seven minutes, it is nearly ten minutes shorter than No. 7, for instance.

Part I, the setting of *Veni, Creator Spiritus*, opens on a chord of E♭ for organ, woodwind and lower strings, followed by the choir's outburst of:

Ex. 20

marked *allegro impetuoso*. Three important themes are at once introduced in this opening passage, which is of elemental strength. Mahler's polyphonic supremacy is demonstrated throughout in a way which entitles him to rank, in terms of technical ability alone, with the Venetian masters of three centuries earlier. Yet from the first entry of the soloists, after the majestic cries of 'Veni', the unmistakable presence of twentieth-century Mahler is felt as he broods over the words: 'Fill with divine grace the hearts of thy creatures.' A modulation from D minor to E major brings the triumphant 'Accende' theme and, eventually, a double fugue in the tempo of a march and an ecstatic *Gloria*. In spite of the introspective central episode, this movement has an irresistible vitality, rushing headlong to its apotheosis.

Part II is nearer to the Mahler world: we seem to have passed into a totally different atmosphere. Now the orchestra comes into its own, setting the Faustian scene—a rocky mountain gorge, with lions prowling—in bleak and remote writing for woodwind over a plodding bass. The connection with the 'Accende' motif is soon established—its three rising notes occur time and again. As the Anchorites softly echo each other, the music becomes richer and the baritone (Pater ecstaticus) invokes 'eternal rapture'; the bass (Pater profundus) has a more dramatic song, vividly accompanied by 'nature music' for the stormy sea and thunderbolts whereby the imagery of love is depicted. With the entry of 'angels, blessed boys, younger angels, and more perfect angels' we are back in the world of the Fourth Symphony until Dr Marianus's (tenor) rapturous plea to the Virgin to unveil herself to the world. An E major chord for harps and harmonium sustains this Lisztian theme, marked *adagissimo*:

Ex.21

132

which begins the final section. The three women, Magna pecca-
trix (soprano), Mulier Samaritana and Maria Aegyptiaca (contraltos) describe Christ's agony and death and plead for Faust's
soul, reinforced by the Penitent (formerly Gretchen), whose
soprano solo is of limpid beauty. The Virgin speaks, and the
work reaches its emotional climax with Marianus's prayer to the
'Virgin, Mother, Queen and Goddess' followed by the final
Mystic Chorus, beginning in hushed awe and ending in a blaze
of E♭ sound and an orchestral coda in which the *Veni, Creator*
theme returns, its interval of the seventh changed into a major
ninth for trumpets and trombones 'as if', Redlich wrote, 'trying
to reach the stars'.

Well, did Mahler reach the stars in this ambitious symphony?
There is no doubt that in a superb performance (such as Solti
has recorded) it can be an overwhelming emotional experience,
temporarily sweeping aside doubts and uncertainties. Even if
the expense of performing it did not ensure its rarity, it is a work
which ought to be reserved for special occasions. Repeated
hearings expose its weaknesses, especially the fitful nature of
Mahler's inspiration. Whereas the more one hears the other
symphonies, the more one comes to admire and understand them
—I can speak only for myself—the Eighth fails to imprint itself
indelibly in the mind. It does not constantly surprise and amaze
the listener, as No. 6 and No. 7 do however familiar they become.
The thematic simplicity and diatonic harmony are not supported
by the sustained inventiveness which alone could have assured
Mahler a total realization of his immense conception. As a
declaration of religious faith I find the Second Symphony more
convincing and moving; as an expression of pantheistic mysticism I find the Third more impressive. Both those works are
more original than No. 8, and are more truly and organically
symphonic, whereas No. 8, especially in Part II, is markedly
episodic and is perhaps best regarded as a series of tableaux or
frescoes. Part I, a magnificent display of Mahler's unrivalled

contrapuntal skill, cannot be wholly absolved of the suggestion that he is saying: 'Just listen to this, all those of you who say I'm an unbridled Romantic megalomaniac.'

The great moments in the work are great indeed: the opening pages, for instance, where one still recaptures the feeling of Mahler's burst of sudden inspiration; the Beethovenian effect (as cruel to the singers too) of the massive double fugue; the spare and sparse scoring of the prelude to Part II (too long, though); and the ecstatic solo arias for Marianus and Gretchen. Where Mahler seems to me to have failed—not surprisingly, really— is in achieving the musical personification of his vision of the Goethean Eternal-Feminine-Alma synthesized with the Platonic Eros. For this he can do no better than the soaring strings and glittering harps of Ex. 21, a beautiful and sensuous passage but perilously near to the idiom of Mascagni and Puccini.[1] It is not, we may be forgiven for thinking, the Mater Gloriosa who 'swims into view', but Santuzza. The artistic judgment which in the other symphonies, particularly No. 4, kept sentimentality at bay by the tartness of the orchestration here temporarily deserted Mahler. Later, after Marianus's final prayer and the chorus's inspired 'Blicket auf', the way to the Mystic Chorus is prepared by another artistic miscalculation—a strange orchestral interlude the texture of which is dominated by the sound of harmonium, pianoforte, celesta, organ, harps and woodwind. It suggests irresistibly a parallel with the spangled interior decoration of certain Austrian Catholic churches, as colourful but as cloying. Musically this is not the Eternal Womanhood that leads us on high, but the Sugar-Plum Fairy on the Christmas tree. Nevertheless, the final chorus, 'Alles Vergängliche', achieves exaltation, although its similarity to the end of the Second Symphony must blunt its impact on experienced Mahlerians.

[1] It is perhaps not without significance that Mahler admired the music of Mascagni and adored Liszt's *Legend of Saint Elizabeth*.

14 *Das Lied von der Erde*

Somewhere in music's pantheon there should be a statue of Father Knight of Worcester, who gave Edward Elgar a copy of Newman's *The Dream of Gerontius* as a wedding present. Alongside it let there be placed a statue of Theobald Pollak, who gave Hans Bethge's *The Chinese Flute* to Mahler. From these gifts arose two masterpieces in which the words acquired an extra dimension and became inseparable from the marvellous music to which they were set.

The genesis of *Das Lied von der Erde* has been described in Chapter 8. In Mahler's depressed state in the summers of 1907 and 1908, when he was suddenly conscious of his physical limitations and therefore exceptionally aware of his mortality, the eighty-three poems which Bethge adapted from English, German and French translations of the Chinese originals aroused profound thoughts and distant echoes. He made certain significant alterations to the text. For example (in *Der Abschied*), Bethge's original has these two lines:

> Die arbeitsamen Menschen
> Geh'n heimwärts, voller Sehnsucht nach dem Schlaf.

> (Labouring men wend homewards,
> Filled with longing for sleep.)

Mahler inserted a phrase from a poem, *Die Nacht blickt mild*, he had written to Johanna Richter in December 1884 so that his version reads:

> Die müden Menschen
> Geh'n heimwärts,

Um im Schlaf vergess'ness Glück
Und Jugend neu zu lernen!

(Tired men wend homewards
to recapture in sleep forgotten happiness and youth.)

It was an alteration symbolic of the mood of nostalgia which the music so perfectly conveys.

Mahler's description of *Das Lied von der Erde* is 'A Symphony for tenor, alto (or baritone) and orchestra'. It is said, by Alma and others, that he was superstitious of a ninth symphony because Beethoven, Schubert, Bruckner and Dvořák had died after completing nine, and that by calling this elaborate symphonic song-cycle a symphony his ninth would be his tenth. One accepts this theory with some reluctance and scepticism because Mahler, great musician that he was, is likely to have realized that although *Das Lied von der Erde* is symphonic, it stands apart from the rest of the series.

Because a work achieves the greatest popularity with the public does not mean that it is its creator's best work. In the case of *Das Lied von der Erde*, however, the public have chosen wisely. It has everything: it is filled with indefinable sadness and longing yet ultimately it is not depressing; it is simple in design; it is fantastically beautifully scored; and it provides the soloists with wonderful opportunities.

So familiar is it today, and so widely admired, that it is easy to overlook its originality and the supreme skill with which it was composed. One of the hallmarks of a masterpiece is that it should appear inevitable, spontaneous. *Das Lied von der Erde* seems continuously new, constantly renewing itself. Yet it represents the culmination of the technique which Mahler had been developing since the First Symphony: perpetual variation, no exact repetitions, and a magical web of melodic counterpoint. The result sounds like a vast inspired improvisation combined with hypersensitive attention to details of tone-colour. He used again the basic ingredients which had supplied him with so much fine music in the past, but here their use was heightened by his response to the poems. He used the intervals of the perfect fourth, the ascending minor third (symbol of space and solitude), the falling second (yearning), and—sole concession to *chinoiserie* —a three-note pentatonic phrase which occurs throughout the work in many permutations, as here in the Finale:

Ex. 22

By masterly deployment of these fragments Mahler gives this work—as he gave other works—a binding unity which subconsciously is communicated to a listener unable to read a note of music and ought to convince those who can that he is a symphonist of the first magnitude. The work is scored for a large, but not mammoth, orchestra, triple woodwind except for five clarinets, and a much enlarged (but most economically used) percussion section to include the exoticism of mandoline, glockenspiel, triangle, cymbals and tambourine. Its first performance was conducted by Walter in Munich in November 1911.

Mahler selected seven of Bethge's poems to make six movements—his first use of this form since the crucial Third Symphony, which has many affinities with *Das Lied von der Erde*, the most obvious being that they both have a long *adagio* as finale preceded by short *intermezzi*. The first movement (*Allegro pesante*) is *Das Trinklied vom Jammer der Erde* (Drinking song of Earth's sorrow), one of Mahler's best constructed and most powerful first movements. The Chinese poem by Li-Tai-Po advocates wine as the best means of coming to terms with the fact that man has less than a hundred years of life in which to delight 'in all the decaying trifles of this earth' (not a theory, incidentally, that Mahler put into practice, because he was abstemious in matters of food and drink). The music begins with a fanfare on the horns, suggesting the defiant desperation of the poem, followed by a burst of manic laughter before the tenor launches into the first of the three stanzas—he needs to be a *Heldentenor* for this notoriously difficult passage, which all too often exposes the weaknesses of the singer's high register in *fortissimo* (the late Fritz Wunderlich pre-eminently showed that it was not a Mahlerian miscalculation). Each stanza ends with the haunting and haunted refrain 'Dunkel ist das Leben, ist der Tod' ('Dark is life, dark is death') which rises a semitone at each appearance (G minor, A flat minor, A minor).

It is soon clear that Mahler is to cover the whole range of emotion and to use every orchestral device (including the remarkable 'flutter-tonguing' by the wind) to heighten the tension. Never did he score more delicately, more imaginatively, more vividly. Never did he draw purer sound from the strings. Sometimes we almost seem to hear the stillness of the air. 'Not all the best of music is in the notes,' he said on one occasion, and in *Das Lied von der Erde* every pause is pregnant. When the tenor sings of the eternal blue sky and the earth blossoming in spring, we can feel Mahler's pulse quicken just as it must have quickened when he first read these words; we can sense how, while composing this music, his fear for his own weakness was conquered and he became extra-sensitively alive to the beauty of the world of nature which had inspired him for so long. 'I am thirstier for life!' It is the eternal wonder of music that it can convey emotion at several different levels simultaneously. Throughout *Das Lied von der Erde* we feel Mahler's hedonism, we feel his rapturous rapport with Nature, we feel his loneliness, his overpowering sense of poignancy at the brevity of man's existence, and we feel his joy in the beauty of the earth and the return of spring. There is nothing nihilistic or defeatist about *Das Lied von der Erde*: its final effect is to uplift the heart. But there are terrors to be faced boldly too: consequently we have

the remarkable passage in this first song where the poet describes
the ape howling on the graves in the moonlight—a passage that
is the musical equivalent of some of the expressionist painting
of the time and takes us momentarily into the world of *Pierrot
Lunaire*.

The second movement is the second longest, *Der Einsame
im Herbst* (The lonely one in autumn), after Tchang-Tsi, like
Li an eighth-century poet. This is a slow movement in D minor;
Mahler's marking is 'somewhat dragging and weary'. It is a
locus classicus for the means by which to obtain a chamber-
music effect from a symphony orchestra: figuration for muted
strings, an oboe like a solitary bird-call, dialogue between horn
and cellos, and the contralto voice sometimes expressionless and
despairing (at the line 'Mein Herz ist müde', 'My heart is weary')
and radiantly ecstatic at the invocation to the 'Sun of Love' to
shine again and dry her tears. The movement ends in gloom
with an orchestral coda of extraordinary beauty pointing the
comparison between human tears and the autumn mists over the
lake with which the movement began.

This is perhaps the place to mention the use of male or female
voice in some of Mahler's works. The baritone is a bracketed
alternative in *Das Lied*, suggesting that Mahler envisaged a
contralto as the norm. It is, nevertheless, fascinating to hear a
baritone in the part, for although the range tests even Fischer-
Dieskau's upper register, there is no doubt that the use of the
male voice intensifies the personal emotional content of the
music—it is as if Mahler himself were singing to us. For this
reason, and also for the subtle changes in tone-colour, some may
always prefer the alternative version, but they will remain a
minority because this is one of the supreme challenges to a contralto or a mezzo-soprano; while singers like Kerstin Thorborg,
Kathleen Ferrier, Christa Ludwig and Janet Baker bring such
interpretative insight to the sheer vocal beauty of this work,
the public will continue to prefer the contrast which the con-

Mahler

tralto and tenor provide. In the case of *Lieder eines fahrenden Gesellen* and *Kindertotenlieder* the choice is less equivocal. It has become the custom—because of the popularity and high standard of contraltos in recent years—for women to sing these works. But both really belong to men, notably the *Kindertotenlieder* in which Mahler himself always preferred a male voice, even engaging a tenor in New York, Ludwig Wüllner (who, incidentally, had sung Elgar's Gerontius in Düsseldorf and London in 1901, 1902 and 1903).

The third, fourth and fifth movements of *Das Lied von der Erde* are short, simply designed miniatures. *Von der Jugend* (Of youth) is in B♭ major. Despite the woodwinds' initial pentatonic scale and the fact that Li-Tai-Po's 'The Porcelain Pavilion' depicts a Chinese scene which everyone knows— willow-pattern, in effect—the flavour of the music is sophisticatedly Viennese. It is all very artificial and mannered, as formal as the mirror-image of the pavilion and the bridge reflected in the pool. Every note, every solo, is polished and precise. The effect is of detached emotion. The fourth movement, *Von der Schönheit* (Of beauty), in G major, is also a Li-Tai-Po poem dealing with another characteristic Chinese scene—girls pick flowers on the river bank; young men on horseback gallop past; and one of them inspires a passionate and longing glance from a girl. For this Mahler provided some of his most graceful and poised music, with an almost fragile orchestral texture except in the riotous outburst of the riders where more than a hint of savagery rises to the surface. The strings make explicit every implication of the girl's glance, and the exquisite piece ends with a kind of berceuse. The mood is broken by the *scherzo*-like fifth movement, in A major, *Der Trunkene im Frühling* (The drunken man in spring). Again Li-Tai-Po commends the merits of drinking, this time to excess. The opening *Allegro* is brittle and strident, essentially light-hearted, but the mood changes poetically when a bird awakens the drunken man and tells him spring has come in the night—a brilliant theme for the piccolo. The fifth verse, mellower and restrained, forms a short trio before the *scherzo* section returns.

Ex. 23

At this point the work has lasted just over thirty minutes. The incomparable finale, *Der Abschied* (The Farewell), is itself to last another thirty. It opens with an unforgettable sound: a low C on cellos, basses, harp, contra-bassoon, horns and gong, above which the oboe cries out in an anguished *gruppetto* which is to dominate the movement (see Ex. 23).

The impression of funereal chill given by this orchestral introduction cannot easily be described, so stark and 'hollow' is the harmony. When the contralto enters above a low C held by the cellos the effect is of a lost soul, an impression intensified by the transference of the oboe's lament to the flute. The poem, by Mong-Kao-Jen, describes sunset and twilight, with the moon 'like a silver bark on the blue lake of heaven'—an aspiring passage in which for the first time warmth floods into the orchestral tone.

The second section is freer, the tonality ambiguous, the voice accompanied by thirds for clarinets and harp. Its principal feature is the long and beautiful introductory oboe solo:

Ex. 24 *Sehr mässig*

which incorporates elements of all the principal motifs of the movement. It becomes an accompaniment to the soloist as she describes the brook singing in the darkness and nature and the world going to sleep, the birds roosting on the branches, while the poet awaits his friend 'to take the last farewell'. The orchestra thins out to nothing but the harp, vibrating in fourths. For the third section the mandoline joins the harp and Mahler introduces the melody for strings which is to dominate the last part of the movement. It is a variant of *Ich bin der Welt*, the idea of longing and the beauty of the earth producing a comparable musical image. The central climax of the first part of the finale is ablaze with ecstasy as the poet longs for his friend to join him. It is no exaggeration to claim that there is no comparable expression in music of the peculiar intensity of longing conveyed in these pages of the score. 'O beauty! O eternal love-and-life-intoxicated world.'

Mahler, for the fourth section, wrote his finest and noblest funeral march as a long interlude between the two poems which constitute the finale. It is constructed from motifs already heard, with the *gruppetto* phrase and the baleful gong as chilly reminders of extinction. As this superbly scored episode sinks into the depth of gloom, the voice re-enters with the first lines of Wang-Wei's poem as recitative. The march rhythm continues, ominous and insistent, while the contralto describes the arrival of the poet's friend and his farewell. At the words 'Du, mein Freund' the compassionate music modulates into the major, and the coda, in C major, begins with the return of the 'Longing' theme, and the soloist sings the words that Mahler himself added:

The dear earth everywhere
Blossoms in spring and grows green again!
Everywhere and eternally the distance shines bright and blue!
Eternally . . . eternally.

This famous passage never loses its miraculous power to grip the listener. As the contralto sings her last words, 'Ewig . . .

ewig', the music fades imperceptibly from our hearing as the orchestration is thinned down to *pianissimo* held chords on the strings, with arpeggios from harp and celesta and the uncanny impersonality of the mandoline. The pentatonic scale which has lent its flavour to the whole work is omnipresent. It is almost always impossible to determine the exact moment when the music ceases, so remote and unearthly are the last bars.

This great *Abschied*, inspired as it is, is very skilfully planned —a cool, calculating brain has controlled music which springs direct from the heart. Mahler's artistic judgment was never surer than in his placing of the orchestral interlude between the poems and in his uncloying use of his fine *Sehnsucht* (longing) theme. If, as has been suggested, the finale of *Die Walküre* was his model, he rose to comparable heights.

Das Lied von der Erde is Mahler's supreme masterpiece because he, who was essentially a programmatic composer however much he may have wished to deny this, found in it the ideal programme for the projection of his musical character and capability. It is music filled with his love of life, a love sharpened to the limits of poignancy by awareness of man's mortality and the transitory nature of existence. I do not find it morbid with death-obsession. As in the Sixth Symphony, he brought to its composition an element of artistic objectivity and detachment while at the same time being gripped by intense emotion. When he said of the *Abschied* to Bruno Walter, 'Is it at all bearable? Will it drive people to do away with themselves?' he knew that he had achieved his aim of expressing a passionate longing for life, not for death. If, through some unimaginable folly, it were to be decreed that only one work by each composer should survive, there could be no hesitation about preserving *Das Lied von der Erde*. It is the best of Mahler, his speaking likeness; and admirers of the work have only to hear a fragment of it to be transported at once into its unique atmosphere. It becomes part of one's metabolism.

15 Symphonies 9 and 10

Mahler's last two symphonies and *Das Lied von der Erde* are already barnacled with romantic mythology. Because they were performed for the first time after his death, because he died comparatively young, leaving a beautiful young widow (and, better still, an unfinished symphony), because he regarded them as excessively difficult to conduct, and because he had been under medical sentence of death, they have invited every kind of subjective interpretation, to some extent justified by their elegiac nature. While I would not suggest that the subject of death was not present in his mind from 1908, I doubt if it obsessed him to the pitch of morbid superstition which has led to statements that he dreaded the idea of performances of *Das Lied von der Erde* and the Ninth Symphony. I do not believe there is any portentous significance in the fact that Mahler did nothing to promote performances of these two works. Here are the practicalities:

Because of the circumstances of his life and the customary difficulties involved in performing new works, especially elaborate and expensive ones for huge orchestras, Mahler was accustomed to long intervals between completion, and sometimes publication, of his works and their first performances, nor does he seem to have been unduly worried about this. The act of creation was the important part for him—once a symphony was finished, all his energies were devoted to sketching the next one and to scoring and re-scoring the completed work. Also, there is every indication that during his decade in Vienna he was determined to avoid any accusation that he used his position to have his symphonies performed. So No. 3, completed 1896, published 1898, waited until 1902; No. 4, completed 1900, was quicker—1901; No. 5, completed 1902, was first played late in 1904; No. 6, scored in 1905, performed 1906; No. 7, finished 1905, first performance 1908; No. 8, composed 1906–7, performed 1910.

From 1908 Mahler divided his time between New York and Europe. He could no longer call on the services of the Vienna Philharmonic to play through his works. But by now he was hearing his symphonies magnificently played by Mengelberg's Concertgebouw Orchestra, and this led him to revise several of them thoroughly. Symphonies 3, 5, 6 and 7 were revised between 1907 and 1909. Symphony No. 2 was revised in 1910, so was No. 4. All this took time. He did not finish scoring *Das Lied von der Erde* until 1909 and the Ninth Symphony until the spring of 1910, whereupon he immediately began to compose No. 10 and to devote four months to rehearsals for No. 8, which meant so much to him. In addition to this, he had the responsibility of re-forming and training the New York Philharmonic, choosing its programmes, rehearsing them, and studying the works by other composers which he was conducting for the first time. It must have disappointed him that he judged the American orchestra incapable of doing justice to his later, more complex works, and the audience incapable of appreciating them. 'I have made up my mind not to start in New York with a performance of the Seventh,' he wrote to Alma in 1909. 'The Seventh is too complicated for a public which knows nothing of me.' It is unlikely, then, that he would have considered a New York first performance for a work of his last period. None of this suggests the outlook of a neurotic. It suggests the sensible attitude of a busy man and of a conscientious musician who had even contemplated cancelling the first performance of No. 8 because, as he wrote to his wife, 'I am absolutely determined *not* to put up with artistic sloppiness'. If he had been obsessed merely with hearing it before he died, he would have put up with anything.

Nor can the argument be sustained that Mahler's inspiration failed him in his last two years. The long first movement of the Ninth Symphony (twenty-six out of seventy-six minutes) is his most advanced and original instrumental movement. Here is the epitome of Mahler's duality, essential Romanticism combining with amazing anticipations of the developments of the next and later generations. This great movement is sufficient testimony to why the evolutionary Mahler has had a greater influence than the revolutionary Schoenberg. In it we hear the sparse, fragmentary textures of Webern, the epigrammatic style of Berg, the 'total thematicism' of Schoenberg. The music has linear complexity and rich polyphony, and its shape is peculiar to Mahler: a combination of sonata-form and rondo with elements of the 'perpetual variation' technique. The principal theme of the movement, a nostalgic D major melody based on two falling seconds and marked *andante comodo* (a leisurely walking-pace), returns several times, as a rondo theme does. It is a significant theme, because it is related intentionally to the 'farewell' *leit-motif* of Beethoven's 'Les Adieux' sonata Op. 81a—the work which had been his 'passport' to the Vienna Conservatory—and at one point is varied to become a pathetic transformation of a Johann Strauss waltz, 'Enjoy life' (*Freut euch des Lebens*, Op. 340).

This idea of farewell was obviously carried over from *Das Lied von der Erde*, for the symphony opens with the tolling of the harp which had dominated *Der Abschied* (an even more direct allusion occurs in the finale) and with a faltering rhythmic phrase for cellos which Leonard Bernstein has suggested may represent Mahler's erratic pulse-beat. This is plausible because the conviction grows that this movement recollects, in intermittent tranquillity, Mahler's emotional crisis at Toblach in 1908 when he had to adapt himself to a new pace of life. No wonder 'Enjoy life' is quoted so wistfully.

The movement is marvellously full of contrast: Romantic nostalgia, as when the principal subject first returns (a passage above which Mahler scribbled in the short score 'O vanished days of youth! O scattered love'), tragic (heroic) defiance, uncanny quiet, a desperate climax, muted trumpet fanfares, and a prophetic and remarkable coda when the orchestra is reduced to a small group of solo instruments toying with fragments of themes and a solo horn takes us back to a simpler musical world while the 'farewell' theme slowly disintegrates. So profoundly had Mahler been stirred by the Bethge poems that clearly he felt that the symphonic song-cycle had not exhausted their musical possibilities: the Ninth Symphony is therefore an extension of *Das Lied*, almost a symphonic commentary upon it. How strongly this is conveyed is evident from Alban Berg's reaction, expressed in a letter to his wife in the summer of 1910. Mahler had lent him the score. 'The first movement is the most heavenly thing Mahler ever wrote,' Berg said. 'It is the expression of an exceptional fondness for this earth, the longing to live in peace on it, to enjoy nature to its depths—before death comes. For he comes irresistibly. The whole movement is permeated by premonitions of death.'

Deryck Cooke has suggested that Mahler took Tchaikovsky's *Pathétique* Symphony as a model for the Ninth. Where the Russian followed his impassioned first movement with a waltz, Mahler returned to the pastoral *Ländler* which had served him well for light relief. For this movement is certainly light relief, even if presented with a heavy touch (it is marked 'rather clumsy and rough'). Those who perceive death in every bar of this symphony easily find a nightmarish quality in the humour —the condemned man eating a hearty breakfast, I suppose. But if we regard it solely from its place in the symphonic scheme, we may see that Mahler had still not quite, but almost wholly, exhausted the musical possibilities of satirical *Ländlers*. The dance-themes are decked out in orchestration that is sometimes witty, sometimes grotesque, sometimes bizarre. There are two trios, in different *tempi*, the first a quick waltz, the second gentle and lilting, its theme based on the falling seconds of the first movement. The coda is Mahler at his spookiest, with the hollow sound of the horn as a spectral intruder.

For his third movement Tchaikovsky wrote his most brilliant march. Mahler too introduces a march tune into his novel Rondo-Burleske. This is in A minor like the first movement of *Das Lied*, which it resembles. Mahler dedicated this movement privately 'to my brothers in Apollo', implying a sarcastic parody of those who accused him of lack of contrapuntal skill. Its marking is 'very defiantly' and that is how it sounds—harsh, disjointed music built on short thematic cells, the first of which echo figures from the second and third movements of the Fifth Symphony. When the trio section returns, it contains a parody of the march from the first movement of the Third—thus does Mahler continue to bind his works into one vast unity:

Ex. 25

The prevailing high pitch of the movement is relaxed by a return to D major when first the trumpet, then the strings, transform one of the jagged rondo themes into a consoling diatonic theme characterized by its octave fall on B. But this is gradually ousted by the fiercer music, which erupts into a final outburst of savagery.

After this comes the *Adagio* last movement. The key is D flat major (a semitone lower than the first movement) and after

M–6

a short introductory flourish like a cry of despair, the strings play the solemn threnody which contains elements of several previous themes, including the Beethoven quotation and the first trio of the *Ländler scherzo*. As it progresses, this movement prophesies some of the writing by Mahler's heir-apparent, Berg, in its simultaneous use of strings in their highest register and basses at their lowest, and of wisps of theme drifting about in a sparse orchestral texture. But the emotional passion of the strings' main theme is never long absent, alternating in the style of a rondo with the woodwind's concertante episodes. There are references to the *Abschied* of *Das Lied von der Erde* and to the consolatory vision from the Rondo-Burleske, but the most significant cross-reference occurs just before the lingering fade-out when the strings quote, from the fourth of the *Kindertotenlieder*, the phrase associated with the children's imagined dwelling-place 'in the sunshine ... on those heights':

Ex. 26

Is it right, therefore, to regard this movement as Mahler's obituary of himself, the egocentric wringing out the last drop of self-pity? That is the usual, Alma-inspired, view. Might it not be his requiem for his daughter, dead only two years when he began to compose it, and for his long-dead brothers and sisters, an elegy as touching as Berg's for Alma's daughter Manon Gropius in his Violin Concerto? Indeed, are we right to hang the label 'egocentric' round Mahler's neck at every opportunity? Allowing that every creator must give substance to his inner visions through the medium of personal experience, was not Mahler's principal preoccupation not so much his own destiny as that of mankind? He was a compassionate artist. His search for God or redemption is mankind's search. The 'hero' of his First and Second Symphonies is Mankind-Mahler, not merely Gustav Mahler. And are we not guilty of the naïveté of which Mahler is so boringly convicted when we cry 'megalomaniac' because he said to Anna von Mildenburg: 'My Third Symphony mirrors the whole world,' and told Bruno Walter not to bother to look at the mountains of the Salzkammergut because 'I've already composed it all'? Is this not the dedicated composer's joy in creation? Here is the essential Mahler in words he wrote to Alma while he was sketching the Ninth Symphony at Toblach in June 1909:

> The 'works' of this person or that ... are the ephemeral and mortal part of him; but what a man makes of himself—what he becomes through the untiring effort to live and to be—is permanent. ... What we leave behind us is only the husk, the shell. The *Meistersinger*, the Ninth, *Faust*—all of them are only the discarded husk! No more, properly speaking, than our bodies are. I don't mean that artistic creation is superfluous. It is a necessity of men for growth and *joy*, which again is a question of health and creative energy. But what actual need is there of notes?

A great Mahler conductor told me that, notwithstanding the Third and Seventh, he regarded the Ninth as the most difficult of the symphonies, technically and interpretatively. He was perhaps acknowledging that, for all its masterly and close-knit organization, it has a fundamental structural weakness which only the most compelling performance will conceal. There is something top-heavy about it. Nothing, not even the lovely *Adagio*, is on the inspired level of the first movement; and although

Mahler must have intended the Rondo-Burleske to be the balancing weight, there is something artificial and contrived about that movement so that it fails to carry full conviction.

The history of the Tenth Symphony is fascinating. For thirteen years after Mahler's death Alma kept the sketches locked away. In 1924, on advice from Richard Specht, she published them in a 116-page photographic facsimile,[1] though it has since transpired that she did not publish them all. Her twenty-four-year-old son-in-law (husband of Anna Mahler) Ernst Křenek, with some help from Berg and Franz Schalk, prepared a performing version of the first and third movements which was played in Vienna in the autumn of 1924. These movements were published in 1951 (with unacknowledged instrumental retouchings by Zemlinsky and Schalk) by Associated Music Publishers of New York under the editorship of a Berg pupil, Otto Jokl.

In 1960, to mark the centenary of Mahler's birth, the British Broadcasting Corporation performed the nine symphonies and published a booklet about them by Deryck Cooke. He found himself unable to discuss the Tenth on the basis of the two published movements and proceeded to copy the manuscript himself as a means of thorough study. He then proposed a broadcast talk with orchestral illustrations. As he worked on the sketches, he discovered that they were far more than the disconnected assortment of jottings which others had dismissed as making no sense. In his own words, he had deciphered 'not a "might-have-been", but an "almost-is" : five full-length movements in various stages of textural completion, but all sufficiently coherent to add up to a magnificent Symphony in F sharp, a symphony in two parts'. [2] Working with the conductor Berthold Goldschmidt, he was able for the broadcast on 19th December 1960 to offer

[1] Published by the Paul Zsolnay Verlag (Berlin, Vienna, Leipzig).
[2] D. Cooke: 'Mahler's Unfinished Symphony', *The Listener*, 15th December 1960.

the first, third and fifth movements complete and substantial fragments of the second and fourth.

The broadcast had several results. Mr Cooke learned that other performing versions existed, though none has yet been heard; he was urged to complete his task, though Alma forbade re-broadcasts of the programme and any further performances. Three years later, after earnest representations on Mr Cooke's behalf, she lifted the ban, although certain distinguished Mahlerians, among them Bruno Walter and Erwin Ratz, continued to maintain that the symphony should not be performed. However, Mr Cooke was able to complete his performing version when a further forty-three pages of manuscript, including practically all the short score of the second movement, were made available to him. So the work was performed in London in August 1964, and introduced to America by Eugene Ormandy at Philadelphia on 5th November 1965. After that Mr Cooke made further revisions based on later research.

It is important to know what Mr Cooke had to work from. Mahler follows his usual practice of building a full-length sketch in four-stave 'open' score, with some indications of intended orchestration. He left five folders of these sketches, each representing a movement continuous from start to finish. Next he would elaborate this four-stave score into a full-score sketch. Half-way through this process he died and so did not begin the final stage of writing a definitive full score. But he left no doubt of the order of the movements, marking them from I to V in blue pencil on the folders. All that Mr Cooke claims [8] for his 'per-

---

[8] Readers interested in detailed accounts of the reconstruction are referred to three important articles by Mr Cooke from which I quote in this chapter: in *The Listener*, op. cit.; 'Mahler's Tenth Symphony: sonority, texture and substance', *Composer*, No. 16, July 1965, pp. 2–8; and programme-note for Royal Liverpool Philharmonic Society concert, 23rd April 1968.

Extensive discussion *pro* and *con* Mr Cooke's performing version may forming version' is that it represents 'the stage that the Tenth Symphony had reached when Mahler died'. It

cannot in any way be thought of as an intended completion of the symphony. . . . If Mahler had lived to complete the work, he would have elaborated the music considerably, refined and perfected it in a thousand details, expanded or contracted or transposed a passage here or there, and of course clothed it in orchestral sound of a subtlety and vividness beyond all our conjectures.

On this last point, Mr Cooke has emphasized that 'approached purely as a Mahler sound-texture [the symphony] scarcely exists after bar 28 of the second movement (and not fully, in every detail, anywhere)'. Yet he believes he has divined Mahler's essential orchestration to within eighty per cent: 'Mahler conceived his music orchestrally, and his short scores are blueprints of instrumentation; if studied and auralized persistently enough, they score themselves—in essentials.' Was Mr Cooke's, then, a presumptuous undertaking, unjustified on moral and æsthetic grounds, as some still think? No. He believed, and I do, that the music, even in its unrevised state, has

such strength and beauty that it dwarfs into insignificance the few momentary uncertainties about notes and the subsidiary additions, and even survives being presented in conjectural orchestration. After all, the leading thematic line throughout, and something like ninety per cent of the counterpoint and harmony, are pure Mahler, and vintage Mahler at that.

He could have added that Mahler rarely altered the structure of

---

be read in these articles: William Malloch: 'Deryck Cooke's Mahler Tenth: an Interim Report', *Music Review*, Vol. XXIII (1962), pp. 292–304; D. Cooke's letter in reply, *Music Review*, Vol. XXIV (1963), pp. 95–6; and Charles Reid: 'Mahler's Tenth', *Music Review*, Vol. XXVI (1965), pp. 318–325.

a work after he had fully sketched it (as he had the Tenth), only the scoring.

The world of music owes an incalculable debt to Deryck Cooke for three reasons: he has enabled us to hear what must at the lowest estimate be called a remarkable approximation to Mahler's intentions; and he has thereby completely altered the emotional interpretation of Mahler's last year. It is apparent from this symphony that it is wrong to regard Mahler as having died in a mood of valediction, defeated or resigned to the inevitable—assuming, which I do not, that the *Adagio-Finale* of No. 9 is a heartbroken egocentric leave-taking. No. 10 is a symphony which transcends thoughts of death and ends with a gloriously affirmatory and positive assertion of a man's spiritual victory. Thirdly, it establishes beyond doubt that Mahler was entering a new phase, in some ways simpler than the complex Ninth Symphony, yet even more prophetic of the collapse of tonality and, paradoxically, even more insistent upon the Classical-Romantic procedures which had always nurtured him.

There is the subsidiary matter of the imprecations to Alma written on the score which are painful to read because of their anguish and have misled some writers into a belief that the symphony was the work of a near-madman. These messages are connected with the Gropius affair of 1910. Perhaps this symphony reflects that experience, at least in part, but whatever passions swept him, they had no effect on his cool brain. There are many examples of the 'schizophrenia' of creative geniuses, of composers writing comic operas, for instance, while their personal world fell about their ears. Ordinary mortals habitually underestimate the ability of such men to concentrate on their work to the exclusion of all else.

Thanks to Mr Cooke, it can be asserted that the Tenth Symphony is (or was to be) greater than the Ninth: it is better balanced and more thoroughly composed. The design is symmetrical: outer movements of about twenty minutes, *scherzos* (second and fourth) of about eleven minutes and a central movement of just under five minutes. Like the Fifth Symphony, it is in two parts, Part I an *Adagio* followed by *Scherzo I*, Part II an *Allegretto moderato* from which *Scherzo II* and the Finale derive their principal material. The opening *Adagio* is a marvellous elegy, more moving than the Finale of No. 9, its main theme (violas) of Brucknerian breadth and richness of harmony, borne aloft on a pulsing *pizzicato*. But it is not long before the strings are in their upper register, almost at the screaming pitch that occasions Mahler to be labelled neurotic, although it is his obsessive concern for clarity and avoidance of muddy textures that is the musical reason for this stylistic feature (derived from Beethoven). All the European music of the 1920s seems to be stirring in the womb of this movement—*Wozzeck*, *Lulu* and others crying to be born. We are in a different sound-world from the Ninth Symphony. Its tensions and complexities boil up into an astonishing nine-note dissonance for the full orchestra pierced by a high A on the trumpet. A kind of serenity returns in the beautiful coda but one senses that nothing can be quite the same again.

Scherzo I, in F sharp minor, is more successful than its counterpart in the Ninth, its opening dance delightfully rhythmical and Haydn-like, its two trios respectively graceful and nostalgic before the jagged strings bring it to an exuberant end. No ghosts to lay there, but what of the enigmatic little movement that opens Part II and is known as *Purgatorio*? Mahler wrote the words 'Purgatorio or Inferno' on the score of this *Allegretto moderato* in B flat minor, then deleted the last two words. Was this a reference to his state of mind during the matrimonial crisis, or has it some bearing on the music, which is like a ghostly *danse macabre* and uses the *ostinato* accompaniment from his *Wunderhorn* song *Das irdische Leben* (about the child who dies from starvation)? There are sudden irruptions of warmth and a final impassioned question. Mahler wrote what can be taken as an almost perfect description of this movement fourteen years earlier in a letter to Marschalk: [4]

Life with all its everlasting changes . . . becomes a dreadful nightmare, its people reminding you of the dancers in a brightly lit ballroom into which you stare from out in the dark at a distance so great that you cannot hear the music of their dance. Life seems so bereft of all meaning, a travesty of itself, and you might wake from your nightmare with a shout of distaste and horror.

Some have called *Purgatorio* trivial, but its triviality is of the same kind as the short movements of Beethoven's late quartets. It is, whatever its emotional connotation, a vital factor in the design of the symphony. It is followed by *Scherzo II, allegro pesante*, beginning in E minor and ending in D minor. Here Mahler achieved the diabolism which he failed to bring off in the Rondo-Burleske. On the score he wrote: 'The devil dances it with me, madness takes hold of me, cursed one'; and there is a terrifying savagery in this music. But it is not overdone, and the thematic material is more distinctive. A theme from the *Purgatorio* becomes a slow waltz, there is a parody of the central orchestral interlude from the finale of *Das Lied von der Erde* and a direct quotation from that work's first movement where the drinker sings that 'joy and singing wither and die'. The movement ends with a Stravinskyan passage for percussion (timpani, bass drum and cymbals). Its last note is a single funereal crack on a muffled drum.

'Only you know what it means,' he wrote, to Alma, on the score. He was referring to an incident in New York during their first visit (December 1907–April 1908) when they stayed at the Hotel Majestic overlooking Central Park. The cortège of a fireman who had died heroically halted beneath their windows. Before it moved on there was a brief stroke on a muffled drum. Mahler, ever susceptible, watched with tears streaming down

[4] 26th March 1896, from Hamburg.

his cheeks.[5] The drum-stroke opens the finale, which continues the key of D minor. Six times this sound of mortality is heard, while the bass tuba and horns intensify the solemn mood. The tuba's theme is a slow version of the *Purgatorio* dance. A long, sinuous melody for the solo flute, poignant with hope (and derived from the slow waltz of *Scherzo II*), leads the music back to Brucknerian rapture, the strings' warmth suggesting the sun returning in spring. But this new life is cut short by the funeral drum and the tuba's theme. Mahler now introduces a central *Allegro* in which all the *Purgatorio* themes are developed and contrasted with a lyrical 'yearning' theme. The climax of this section is the dissonant chord from the *Adagio* and its trumpet note, followed by a progressively more lyrical and impassioned episode as the music returns to F sharp major and the violas' theme from the *Adagio* becomes a great song of life and love— the most fervently intense ending to any Mahler symphony and a triumphant vindication of his spiritual courage.

Mahler died on the full crest of his creative powers. What would his Eleventh Symphony have been like? Would he have moved further along the path which his followers were to take? Useless to speculate, of course, especially as one fears to think of the effect on such a sensitive man of the carnage of the First World War. But it remains uncanny to think that he would have celebrated his eightieth birthday in 1940, would have heard the great works of Berg, Bartók and Stravinsky and the twelve-note revolution of Schoenberg. He would have seen the rape of his native Czechoslovakia and Austria; and his conversion to Catholicism would not have saved him from permanent exile with so many other Jews.

[5] This incident occurred on Sunday afternoon, 16th February 1908. The funeral was of Charles W. Kruger, Deputy Chief of the City of New York Fire Department, commanding the 2nd Division, who died from injuries received while fighting a fire at 217 Canal Street at 1 a.m. on 14th February. He had been in the fire service for thirty-six years.

Wherein lies Mahler's immense and growing appeal? He is not so easy to listen to as Tchaikovsky; he wrote no concerto with which brilliant executants can display their skill; his brand of nostalgia is not the sensuous heartbreak so marvellously expressed by Delius in *Sea-Drift*, but a spiritual longing for loneliness; he offers us no certainty as a result of his constant search for an answer to the questions which bewildered him: he is often contradictory, and Bruno Walter called his attititude 'desultory'.

But although the emotional and autobiographical elements of Mahler's music should never be left out of account, he must be judged primarily as a musician—and not exclusively as a musician whose anticipation of the future is so remarkable. He must be assessed on what he did, not on what others took and developed from him. After all, even his most advanced passages are basically within the context of the nineteenth century. Taking a hint from Berlioz, he created the orchestral song-cycle, realizing that the complex emotions of Romantic poetry required the resources of an orchestra to do them justice. With *Das Lied von der Erde* he created a new form from which have sprung Britten's *Spring Symphony* and *Nocturne* and Shostakovich's Fourteenth Symphony, to name but three. He showed that the symphony was still a valid and fruitful form, and he did this by expansion, as it were, while his contemporary, Sibelius, also put new life into the symphony by compression. He created an entirely individual sound, unmistakable, inimitable—a Mahler world.

It is true that there is an element of the actor in Mahler, that he strikes attitudes not from conviction but as a spiritual experiment. But the result is never insincere. To some temperaments he will always be anathema because it is felt that he did not subject his musical thought-processes to enough refining self-criticism, that he was too much the suffering human and not sufficiently the detached artist. There is something in this, though study of his scores reveals a musical headwork, as Shaw would have described it, of a peculiarly intricate nature.

'Thrice homeless ... always an intruder,' he said. 'How alien and lonely I feel at times.' This lack of identification with any roots is surely the fundamental cause of the contrasts and conflicts in his music and therefore a source of artistic strength. Born in Bohemia, he developed very differently from his contemporary, the Moravian Janáček. He turns a quizzical, detached musical eye on both the folksongs of his boyhood and the sophisticated Viennese music of his manhood. Yet this sense of alienation in no way detracts from the emotional impact of his music. Its compassion, its humanity, its wry humour, shine through its complexities, its self-questioning, its anguished doubting. Those who love Mahler's music may give a variety of reasons for their love. Common to them all, I believe, would be agreement with Schoenberg: 'I sensed a human being, a drama, *truth*, the most ruthless truth.' In a world of collapsing values Mahler's truth about music and about Mahler is something to cherish.

Appendix A   Calendar

(Figures in brackets denote the age reached by the person mentioned during the year in question)

YEAR	AGE	LIFE	CONTEMPORARY MUSICIANS AND EVENTS
1860		Gustav Mahler born July 7 at Kališt, Bohemia, son of Bernard Mahler (32) and Marie, née Hermann (23). Family move to Jihlava (Iglau) in December.	Wolf born, March 13; Albéniz born, May 29; Charpentier born, June 25; Paderewski born, Nov. 6; Berlioz 57; Bizet 22; Humperdinck 6; Marschner 65; Rossini 68; Smetana 36; J. Strauss (ii) 35; Wagner 47; Brahms (27) signs manifesto against 'the New Music'.
1866	6	Learns piano, goes to school.	Busoni born, April 1; Satie born, May 17; Debussy 4; Delius 4; Elgar 9; Weingartner 3; R. Strauss 2; Nielsen 1; Sibelius 1.
1869	9	Studies under piano-teacher Brosch and himself teaches younger boy.	Vienna Hofoper on Ringstrasse opens, May 25.
1870	10	Gives public recital in Jihlava, Oct. 13.	Lehár born, April 30; Schmitt born, Sept. 28; Pfitzner 1; Franco-Prussian War; first Vienna *Meistersinger*, Feb. 27.

Mahler

YEAR	AGE	LIFE	CONTEMPORARY MUSICIANS AND EVENTS
1871	11	Studying at Prague Gymnasium.	Mengelberg born, March 28; Auber (89) dies, May 12.
1874	14	His brother Ernst (13) dies.	Holst born, Sept. 21; Ives born, Oct. 20; Schoenberg born, Sept. 13; Skriabin 2; Vaughan Williams 2; Zemlinsky 2; Rakhmaninov 1; Reger 1.
1875	15	Enters Vienna Conservatory, Sept. 20. Begins opera *Herzog Ernst von Schwaben.*	Ravel born, March 7; Bizet (36) dies, June 3; Richter (32) becomes conductor, Vienna Hofoper.
1876	16	Wins prizes for piano and composition. Performs in his piano quintet in Vienna, July 10, and Jihlava, Sept. 12, and in his violin sonata, Jihlava, Sept. 12.	Falla born, Nov. 23; Bruno Walter born, Sept. 15; first cycle of *Ring*, Bayreuth, Aug. 13–17; Brahms's Symphony No. 1, first perfs.: Carlsruhe, Nov. 6, Vienna, Dec. 17.
1877	17	Wins another piano prize. Asked by Bruckner (53) to make two-piano arrangephony of his Symphony No. 3.	Dohnányi born, July 27; first Vienna *Walküre*, March 5; Brahms's Symphony No. 2, first perf., Vienna, Dec. 30.
1878	18	Leaves Conservatory, July 11. Matriculates at Jihlava. Gives piano lessons. Begins to write words of cantata *Das klagende Lied*. Attends Vienna University lectures on philosophy and history of painting.	First Vienna performances of *Rheingold*, Jan. 24, and of *Siegfried*, Nov. 9.

YEAR	AGE	LIFE	CONTEMPORARY MUSICIANS AND EVENTS
1879	19	Piano tutor in Hungary and Vienna.	Alma Schindler born, Aug. 31; Medtner born, Dec. 24. First Vienna *Götterdämmerung*, Feb. 14; *Ring*, May 26–30.
1880	20	Three songs composed, Feb. and March. Conducts during summer at Hall spa. Completes *Das klagende Lied*, Nov. 1. Begins opera *Die Argonauten.*	Pizzetti born, Sept. 20.
1881	21	*Das klagende Lied* fails to win Beethoven Prize. Conducts at Laibach. Begins opera *Rübezahl.*	Bartók born, March 25; Mussorgsky (42) dies, March 28.
1882	22	Conducts at Jihlava.	Kodály born, Dec. 16; Stravinsky born, June 17; first perf. of *Parsifal*, Bayreuth, July 25; Berlin Philharmonic Orch. founded.
1883	23	Conducts at Olmütz (Jan.). Visits Bayreuth, July. Appointed second conductor at Cassel court theatre.	Webern born, Dec. 3; Wagner (69) dies, Feb. 13. First perf. of Brahms's Symphony No. 3, Vienna, Dec. 2; first Vienna *Tristan*, Oct. 4.
1884	24	Composes incidental music for *Der Trompeter von Säkkingen*. Begins Symphony No. 1. Composes *Lieder eines fahrenden Gesellen*, Dec.	Smetana (60) dies, May 12; Bruckner's Symphony 7, first perf., Leipzig, Dec. 30.
1885	25	End of his love affair with Johanna Richter. Leaves	Berg born, Feb. 9; Wellesz born, Oct. 21; first perf. of

YEAR	AGE	LIFE	CONTEMPORARY MUSICIANS AND EVENTS
		Cassel post, July 1. Appointed second conductor, Deutsches Landestheater, Prague. Notable success as interpreter of Wagner and Mozart operas.	Brahms's Symphony No. 4, Meiningen, Oct. 25.
1886	26	Three songs performed at Prague, April. Second conductor (under Nikisch) at Leipzig, Aug.	Liszt (74) dies, July 31. R. Strauss conductor at Meiningen.
1887	27	Conducts first *Siegfried* at Leipzig. Works on completing Weber's *Die drei Pintos*. Affair with Mathilde von Weber. Meets R. Strauss in Leipzig, autumn. Completing Symphony No. 1.	First perf. of Verdi's *Otello* Milan, Feb. 5.
1888	28	First perf. *Die drei Pintos*, Leipzig, Jan. 20. Resigns Leipzig post, May. Becomes musical director, Budapest opera. Begins Symphony No. 2.	Alkan (74) dies, March 29.
1889	29	Father dies, Feb. 18 and mother, Oct. 4. Symphony No. 1 first perf. Budapest, Nov. 20 (under title Symphonic Poem).	N. Cardus born, April 2; Boult born, April 8. First perf. of Strauss's *Don Juan*, Weimar, Nov. 11.
1890	30	Holiday in Italy with his sister Justine.	Franck (67) dies, Nov. 8.
1891	31	After quarrel with new Budapest Intendant, M.	Prokofiev born, April 23.

YEAR	AGE	LIFE	CONTEMPORARY MUSICIANS AND EVENTS
		resigns, March 14. Begins as chief conductor, Hamburg, March 29. Plays part of Symphony No. 2 to Hans von Bülow.	
1892	32	Visit to London as conductor, June and July. Vols. I, II and III of *Lieder und Gesänge* published. Songs with orchestra performed in Hamburg and Berlin.	First perf. of Bruckner's Symphony No. 8, Vienna, Dec. 18.
1893	33	Spends summer at Steinbach-am-Attersee where he works on Symphony No. 2. Symphony No. 1 performed in Hamburg, Oct. 27.	Tchaikovsky (53) dies, Nov. 6; first perf. of Verdi's *Falstaff*, Milan, Feb. 9.
1894	34	Symphony No. 1 (with subtitle *Titan*) performed Weimar Festival, June 29; Symphony No. 2 completed, Steinbach, July 25. Succeeds Bülow as conductor of Hamburg symphony concerts.	Bülow (63) dies, Feb. 12; first perf. of Bruckner's Symphony, No. 5, Graz, April 8.
1895	35	His brother Otto shoots himself, Feb. M. conducts first three movements of Symphony No. 2, Berlin, March 4, and complete Symphony, Berlin, Dec. 13. Begins Symphony No. 3 at Steinbach in summer.	Hindemith born, Nov. 16; first perf. of Strauss's *Till Eulenspiegel*, Cologne, Nov. 5.
1896	36	First performance of *Lieder*	Bruckner (72) dies, Oct.

YEAR	AGE	LIFE	CONTEMPORARY MUSICIANS AND EVENTS
		eines fahrenden Gesellen and four-movement version of Symphony No. 1, Berlin, March 16. Completes Symphony No. 3, Steinbach, Aug. 6.	11; R. Strauss becomes chief conductor at Munich.
1897	37	Becomes Roman Catholic, Feb. 23. Tour of Russia, March. Leaves Hamburg. Engaged as *Kapellmeister*, Vienna Hofoper, May 1; deputy director, July 13, director, Oct. 8. *Lieder eines fahrenden Gesellen* and Symphony No. 2 published.	Brahms (63) dies, April 3.
1898	38	Intensive work at Vienna Opera. Becomes conductor, Vienna Philharmonic, after Richter. Revises some of his works. Operation for haemorrhoids in June.	R. Strauss (34) becomes principal conductor, Berlin Opera, and composes *Ein Heldenleben.*
1899	39	Buys land for a house at Maiernigg (Wörthersee). Begins Symphony No. 4 in Aug. at Alt-Aussee (Styria) and composes songs.	Poulenc born, Jan. 7; Barbirolli born, Dec. 2; J. Strauss (ii) (73) dies, June 3; first perf. of Elgar's *Enigma Variations*, London, June 19; Richter settles in Manchester, Oct.
1900	40	Takes Vienna Philharmonic to Paris, June. Completes Symphony No. 4 at Maiernigg, Aug. 5.	Copland born, Nov. 14; Křenek born, Aug. 23; Weill born, March 2; first perfs. of Puccini's *Tosca*, Rome, Jan. 14, Charpen-

YEAR	AGE	LIFE	CONTEMPORARY MUSICIANS AND EVENTS
			tier's *Louise*, Paris, Feb. 2, and Elgar's *Dream of Gerontius*, Birmingham, Oct. 3.
1901	41	Conducts first performance *Das klagende Lied*, Vienna, Feb. 17. Resigns conductorship, Vienna Philharmonic, April. Begins Symphony No. 5 at Maiernigg, summer, also composes Rückert settings including three of *Kindertotenlieder*. Meets Alma Schindler, Nov. 7. M. conducts first performance of Symphony No. 4 in Munich, Nov. 25.	Verdi (87) dies, Jan. 27; first complete perf. of Debussy's *Nocturnes*, Paris, Oct. 27.
1902	42	Conducts first Vienna performances of Symphony No. 4 on Jan. 12 and 20. Marries Alma Schindler, March 9. Honeymoon while conducting in Russia. Conducts first performance Symphony No. 3, Crefeld, June 9. Meets Mengelberg. Symphony No. 5 completed, summer. Daughter Maria born, Nov. 3.	Walton born, March 29. First perfs. of Debussy's *Pelléas et Mélisande*, Paris, April 30, Schoenberg's *Verklärte Nacht*, Vienna, March 18, and Nielsen's Symphony No. 2, Copenhagen, Dec. 1.
1903	43	Increasing number of performances of Mahler's symphonies in Germany, many conducted by him. Association with stage designer	Wolf (42) dies, Feb. 22. Wood conducts first English perf. of a Mahler symphony (1), London, Oct. 21. First perf. of Bruckner's

167

YEAR	AGE	LIFE	CONTEMPORARY MUSICIANS AND EVENTS
		Alfred Roller begins with *Tristan*, Vienna, Feb. 21. Begins Symphony No. 6, Maiernigg. Conducts Symphony No. 3, Amsterdam, Oct. 22 and 23.	No. 9, Vienna, Feb. 11.
1904	44	Daughter Anna born, June 15. Completes Symphony No. 6 at Maiernigg, Sept. 9. Begins Symphony No. 7. Rückert settings completed. Conducts famous *Fidelio* production, Oct. 7, and first performance Symphony No. 5, Cologne, Oct. 18.	Dvořák (62) dies, May 1; Hanslick (78) dies, Aug. 6. First perfs. of Bartók's *Kossuth*, Budapest, Jan. 13; Janáček's *Jenufa*, Brno, Jan. 21; Sibelius's violin concerto, Helsinki, Feb. 8; Puccini's *Madama Butterfly*, Milan, Feb. 17; R. Strauss's *Symphonia Domestica*, New York, March 21; Ravel's *Shéhérazade*, Paris, May 17. First American perf. of a Mahler symphony (4) conducted by W. Damrosch, New York, Nov. 6.
1905	45	First performance of *Kindertotenlieder*, Vienna, Jan. 29. Conducts his symphonies on several occasions. Completes Symphony No. 7 in summer. Notable Vienna revival of *Don Giovanni*, Dec. 21. Symphony No. 5, *Kindertotenlieder* and *Rückertlieder* published.	Tippett born, Jan. 2. First perfs. of Schoenberg's *Pelléas et Mélisande*, Vienna, Jan. 26; Debussy's *La Mer*, Paris, Oct. 15; Strauss's *Salome*, Dresden, Dec. 9; and Lehár's *Merry Widow*, Vienna, Dec. 30.

YEAR	AGE	LIFE	CONTEMPORARY MUSICIANS AND EVENTS

1906 46 Conducts Mozart revivals of *Seraglio*, Jan. 29, and *Figaro*, March 30. Conducts first performance of Symphony No. 6, Essen, May 27. Symphony No. 6 published. Composes Symphony No. 8, Maiernigg, June–Aug. Conducts at Salzburg in Aug.

Shostakovich born, Sept. 25. First perf. of Delius's *Sea-Drift*, Essen, May 24.

1907 47 Heart lesion diagnosed. Daughter Maria dies, July 5. Resigns from Vienna Hofoper, Aug.; accepts contract for Metropolitan, New York. Conducts last opera (*Fidelio*) in Vienna, Oct. 15; leaves for concerts in St Petersburg, Oct., and Helsinki, Nov., where he meets Sibelius. Conducts last concert in Vienna (his Symphony No. 2) Nov. 24. Sails for New York, Dec.

Grieg (64) dies, Sept. 4. First perf. of Schoenberg's String Quartet No. 1, Vienna, Feb. 15, and Sibelius's Symphony No. 3, Helsinki, Sept. 25.

1908 48 Début at Metropolitan, New York, in *Tristan*, Jan. 1. During summer at Toblach composes *Das Lied von der Erde*. Conducts first performance of Symphony No. 7, Prague, Sept. 19. Returns to New York Metropolitan and also con-

Messiaen born, Dec. 10; Rimsky-Korsakov (64) dies, June 21. First perfs. of Delius's *Brigg Fair*, Liverpool, Jan 18; Rakhmaninov's Symphony No. 2, Moscow, Nov. 8; Elgar's Symphony No. 1, Manchester, Dec. 3; and Schoen-

YEAR	AGE	LIFE	CONTEMPORARY MUSICIANS AND EVENTS
		ducts N.Y. Symphony Orchestra in his Symphony No. 2 on Dec. 8.	berg's String Quartet No. 2, Vienna, Dec. 21.
1909	49	Severs connection with Metropolitan. Accepts 3-year contract as conductor of reorganized New York Philharmonic. Returns to Europe for summer. Sits to Rodin in Paris. Begins Symphony No. 9 at Toblach and Göding. Returns to New York for first Philharmonic season (46 concerts). Conducts Symphony No. 1 on Dec. 16.	Albéniz (48) dies, May 18. First perfs. of Strauss's *Elektra*, Dresden, Jan 25, Bartók's Suite No. 2, Budapest, Nov. 22, and Rakhmaninov's Piano Concerto No. 3, New York (Damrosch), Nov. 28. Schoenberg completes *Drei Klavierstücke*, Op. 11, on Aug. 7.
1910	50	Takes N.Y. Philharmonic on tour. Completes Symphony No. 9. Conducts Symphony No. 2 in Paris, April; conducts in Rome in May; begins Symphony No. 10 at Toblach. Alma in sanatorium and precipitates marital crisis through friendship with Walter Gropius. M. consults Freud at Leyden in Aug. Conducts first two performances of Symphony No. 8 at Munich, Sept. 12 and 13. Revises Symphonies Nos. 2 and 4. His second N.Y. Phil-	Balakirev (73) dies, May 29. First perfs. of Debussy's *Rondes de Printemps*, Paris, March 2; Bartók's String Quartet No. 1, Budapest, March 19; Stravinsky's *Fire-Bird*, Paris, June 25; and Elgar's Violin Concerto, London, Nov. 10.

YEAR	AGE	LIFE	CONTEMPORARY MUSICIANS AND EVENTS
		harmonic season opens on Nov. 1.	
1911	50	Conducts Symphony No. 4 in New York, Jan. 17 and 20. After conducting on Feb. 21 he is seriously ill with severe streptococcal blood infection. Returns to Paris for serum treatment in April. Taken to sanatorium in Vienna, where he dies, May 18. Bruno Walter conducts first performance of *Das Lied von der Erde* at Munich on Nov. 20.	First perfs. of Strauss's *Der Rosenkavalier*, Dresden, Jan. 26; Skriabin's *Prometheus*, Moscow, March 15; and Sibelius's Symphony No. 4, Helsinki, April 3. Josef Stransky appointed conductor of New York Philharmonic, May 17.

Appendix B   Catalogue of Works

SONGS

1880   Three Songs for tenor and pianoforte (words by Mahler)
1. *Im Lenz* (19 Feb.)
2. *Winterlied* (27 Feb.)
3. *Maitanz im Grünen* (5 March)—see also *Hans und Grethe* below

All that survive of a projected Five Songs 'dedicated to Josephine'.
First performance: Zdenek Knittl (tenor), Alfred Rosé (pianoforte),
Brno Radio, 30 Sept. 1934.

1880–3   Five Songs for voice and pianoforte
1. *Frühlingsmorgen* (Leander)
2. *Erinnerung* (Leander)
3. *Hans und Grethe* (Mahler)
4. *Serenade aus 'Don Juan'* (Tirso de Molina)
5. *Phantasie aus 'Don Juan'* (Tirso de Molina)

No. 3 is same song as *Maitanz im Grünen*. First perf.: Prague, 20
April 1886, Betty Frank (soprano), accompanied by Mahler. These
Five Songs were published as Book I of the *Lieder und Gesänge aus
der Jugendzeit* by Schott, Mainz in February 1892. Books II and III,
all with words from *Des Knaben Wunderhorn*, were published at the
same time, but were composed between 1888 and 1891:

II.   6. *Um schlimme Kinder artig zu machen*
7. *Ich ging mit Lust durch einen grünen Wald*
8. *Aus! Aus!*
9. *Starke Einbildungskraft*
III. 10. *Zu Strassburg auf der Schanz*
11. *Ablösung im Sommer*
12. *Scheiden und Meiden*

13. *Nicht Wiedersehen!*
14. *Selbstgefühl*

1884 *Lieder eines fahrenden Gesellen*, for voice and orchestra (or pianoforte). Words by Mahler. Composed in November and December of 1884. Revised *c.* 1892, further revised 1896, published 1897 (Vienna, Weinberger). Orchestral version published 1912.

1. *Wenn mein Schatz Hochzeit macht*
2. *Ging heut' Morgen übers Feld*
3. *Ich hab' ein glühend Messer*
4. *Die zwei blauen Augen*

First perf.: Berlin, 16 March 1896, Anton Sistermans (baritone), Berlin Philharmonic Orchestra (Mahler); first perf. in Britain: Queen's Hall, London, 3 Nov. 1927,[1] Maria Olczewska (contralto), Orchestra of Royal Philharmonic Society (Sir Henry Wood).

1888–99 *Lieder aus 'Des Knaben Wunderhorn'*, for voice and orchestra (or pianoforte). Originally named *Humoresken*. Published 1899 (Vienna, Weinberger). Dates of composition, where known, in brackets.

I. 1. *Der Schildwache Nachtlied* (1892)
  2. *Verlor'ne Müh'* (1892)
  3. *Trost im Unglück* (6 April 1892)
  4. *Wer hat dies Liedlein erdacht?* (1892)
  5. *Das irdische Leben* (1893)

II. 6. *Des Antonius von Padua Fischpredigt* (Steinbach, 1 Aug. 1893)
  7. *Rheinlegendchen* (originally *Tanzlegendchen*) (Steinbach, 10 Aug. 1893)
  8. *Lied des Verfolgten im Turm* (1895)
  9. *Wo die schönen Trompeten blasen* (1895)
  10. *Lob des hohen Verstandes* (21 June 1896)
  11. *Es sungen drei Engel* (Symphony No. 3) (1895)
  12. *Urlicht* (Symphony No. 2) (1892–4)

---

[1] This date is speculative. This cycle and *Kindertotenlieder* were scheduled for performance at a Promenade Concert on 17 October 1914, but it was cancelled.

First perf. of Nos. 1 and 2 Berlin, 12 Dec: 1892, Amalie Joachim
(mez.-sop.), Berlin Philharmonic cond. Raphael Maszkowski; of
Nos. 3, 4, 7, Hamburg, 27 Oct. 1893, Clementine Schuch-Prosska
(soprano) and Paul Bulss (baritone), with orchestra (Mahler); of
Nos. 5 and 9, Vienna, 14 Jan. 1900, Selma Kurz (soprano), Vienna
Philharmonic (Mahler); and of Nos. 6 and 8 Vienna, 29 Jan. 1905,
F. Weidemann (baritone) and orch. (Mahler). Other settings from
Des Knaben Wunderhorn:

> *Wir geniessen die himmlischen Freuden* (Symphony No. 4). For
> soprano and orchestra (12 March 1892)
>
> *Revelge* (1899). Published 1905 (Leipzig, Kahnt)
>
> *Der Tamboursg'sell* (July 1901). Published 1905 (Leipzig, Kahnt)

1901–4 *Kindertotenlieder* (Rüchert), for voice and orchestra (or
pianoforte). Published 1905 (Leipzig, C. F. Kahnt Nachfolger).

1. *Nun will die Sonn' so hell aufgeh'n* (1901)
2. *Nun seh' ich wohl* (1901)
3. *Wenn dein Mütterlein* (1901)
4. *Oft denk' ich, sie sind nur ausgegangen* (1904)
5. *In diesem Wetter* (1904)

First perf.: Vienna, 29 Jan. 1905. Friedrich Weidemann (baritone)
and orchestra (Mahler); first perf. in Britain: Bechstein Hall,
London, 28 May 1913 (with pianoforte), Lula Mysz- Gmeiner (con-
tralto), Richard Epstein (pianoforte); with orchestra, 27 May 1924,
Elena Gerhardt (contralto), L.S.O. (Fritz Reiner); first U.S. perf.:
New York, 26 January 1910, Ludwig Wüllner (tenor), N.Y.P.O.
(Mahler).

Fünf Lieder nach Rückert (Five Rückert Songs) for voice and orchestra (or pianoforte). Published 1905 (Leipzig, C. F. Kahnt Nachf.).

1. *Ich atmet' einen linden Duft* (1901)
2. *Liebst du um Schönheit* (1902)
3. *Blicke mir nicht in die Lieder* (1901)
4. *Ich bin der Welt abhanden gekommen* (1901)
5. *Um Mitternacht* (1901)

First perf.: Vienna, 29 Jan. 1905 (excluding No. 2). F. Weidemann
(baritone) and orch. (Mahler).

CANTATA

1878–80   *Das klagende Lied* (words by Mahler) for soprano, contralto, tenor, bass, chorus and orchestra. Original version in three parts completed 1 Nov. 1880: I *Waldmärchen*, II *Der Spielmann*, III *Hochzeitstück*.

Revised 1888 into two parts, *Waldmärchen* being deleted. Scoring further revised 1893, 1898–9, post-1900. Publication of revised version, 1902 (Vienna, Weinberger). First perf.: Vienna, 17 Feb. 1901, Vienna Philharmonic Orchestra and choir of Vienna *Singakademie* (Mahler) with Elise Elizza, Anna von Mildenburg,[2] Edyth Walker and Fritz Schrödter; first perf. in Britain: Royal Festival Hall, London, 13 May 1956, London Symphony Orchestra, Goldsmiths' Choral Union (Walter Goehr) with Joan Sutherland, Norma Procter, Peter Pears.

Original version: first perf. of *Waldmärchen* alone, Brno Radio, 28 Nov. 1934 (in Czech) conducted by Alfred Rosé; first perf. of complete original version: Vienna Radio 8 April 1935 conducted by Alfred Rosé; in Britain, Royal Festival Hall, London, 21 April 1970, L.S.O. and Chorus (Pierre Boulez) with Elisabeth Söderström, Grace Hoffman, Ernst Häfliger; first U.S. performance: New Haven, 13 Jan. 1970, New Haven S.O. (Frank Brieff), Veronica Tyler (soprano), Janet Baker (mez.-soprano), Blake Stern (tenor), Richard McKee (bass).

SONG-SYMPHONY

1907–9   *Das Lied von der Erde*, Symphony for alto (or baritone), tenor and orchestra (words by Hans Bethge, based on Chinese poems, with additions by Mahler). Published 1911 (Vienna, U.E.).

First perf.: Munich, 20 Nov. 1911, Mme Charles Cahier (contralto), William Miller (tenor), Orchestra of Munich Concert Society (Bruno Walter); first performance in Britain: Queen's Hall, London, 31 Jan. 1914, Doris Woodall, Gervase Elwes and Queen's

[2] Two sopranos shared soprano role.

Hall Orchestra (Wood); first U.S. perf.: Philadelphia, 14 Dec. 1916, Philadelphia Orchestra (Stokowski).

SYMPHONIES

1884–8 Symphony No. 1 in D major. Revised 1893, 1896 (reduced from five to four movements) and 1897–8. Published 1899 (Vienna, Weinberger).

First perf.: Budapest, 20 Nov. 1889 (Mahler); first perf. in Britain: Queen's Hall, London, 21 Oct. 1903, Queen's Hall Orchestra (Wood); first U.S. perf.: New York, 16 Dec. 1909, N.Y.P.O. (Mahler).
First 20th-century perf. of five-movement version: New Haven, 9 April 1968, New Haven S.O. (Frank Brieff); first perf. in Britain of *Blumine* movement: Aldeburgh, 18 June 1967, L.S.O. (Britten).

1888–94 Symphony No. 2 in C minor. For soprano, contralto, mixed chorus and orchestra. Revised 1910. Published 1897 (Leipzig, Hofmeister).

First perf.: first three movements only, Berlin, 4 March 1895, Berlin Philharmonic Orchestra (Mahler); complete, Berlin, 13 Dec. 1895, Berlin Philharmonic (Mahler), with Josephine von Artner (soprano), Hedwig Felden (contralto); first perf. in Britain: Queen's Hall, London, 16 April 1931, Queen's Hall Orchestra and Chorus (Bruno Walter), with Luise Helletsgruber (soprano), Enid Szanto (contralto); first U.S. perf.: New York, 8 Dec. 1908, N.Y. Symphony Orchestra (Mahler), with Laura L. Combs (soprano) and Gertrude Stein Bailey (contralto).

1895–6 Symphony No. 3 in D minor. For contralto, women's chorus, boys' chorus and orchestra. Published 1898 (Vienna, Weinberger).

First perf.: Crefeld, 9 June 1902 (Mahler) at festival of All-gemeine Deutsche Musikverein; first perf. in Britain: B.B.C. broadcast, 29 Nov. 1947, B.B.C. Symphony Orchestra, Chesham Ladies' Choir, boys of London Choir School (Sir Adrian Boult) with Kathleen Ferrier (contralto); (public) London, St Pancras Town Hall, 28 Feb. 1961, Polyphonia Symphony Orchestra, Wimbledon

Girls' Choir, William Ellis School boys' choir (Bryan Fairfax), with Jean Evans (contralto); first U.S. perf.: New York, 8 Feb. 1922, New York Philharmonic (Mengelberg).

1899–1900   Symphony No. 4 in G major. For soprano and orchestra, Revised 1910. Published 1902 (Vienna, Waldheim-Eberle).

First perf.: Munich, 25 Nov. 1901 (Mahler), with Margarete Michalek (soprano); first perf. in Britain: Queen's Hall, London, 25 Oct. 1905, Mrs Henry J. Wood (soprano) and Queen's Hall Orchestra (Wood); first U.S. perf.: New York, 6 Nov. 1904, N.Y. Symphony Orchestra (Walter Damrosch), with Mme de Montjau (soprano).

1901–2   Symphony No. 5 in C sharp minor.[3] Revised 1904, 1905, 1907, 1909. Published 1905 (Leipzig, C. F. Peters).

First perf.: Cologne, 18 Oct. 1904 (Mahler); first perf. in Britain: Stoll Theatre, London, 21 Oct. 1945, London Philharmonic Orchestra (Heinz Unger); *Adagietto* only: Queen's Hall, London, 31 Aug. 1909, Queen's Hall Orchestra (Wood); first U.S. perf.: Cincinnati, 25 March 1905, Cincinnati S.O. (Frank van der Stucken).

1903–5   Symphony No. 6 in A minor. Revised 1908. Published 1906 (Leipzig, C. F. Kahnt Nachf.).

First perf.: Essen, 27 May 1906 (Mahler), festival of Allgemeine Deutsche Musikverein; first British broadcast (Hamburg perf.) 31 Dec. 1947; first British orch. broadcast: 28 Dec. 1950, B.B.C. Symphony Orchestra (Walter Goehr); first U.S. performance: New York, 11 Dec. 1947, N.Y.P.O. (Dmitri Mitropoulos).

1904–5   Symphony No. 7 in B minor. Revised 1909. Published 1908 (Berlin, Bote und Bock).

First perf.: Prague, 19 Sept. 1908 (Mahler); first perf. in Britain: Queen's Hall, London, 18 Jan. 1913, Queen's Hall Orchestra (Wood); first U.S. perf.: Chicago, 15 April 1921, Chicago S.O. (Frederick Stock).

1906–7   Symphony No. 8 in E flat major. For 8 soloists (3 sopranos, 2 contraltos, tenor, baritone and bass), mixed chorus, boys' chorus

---

[3] The keys given for this symphony and Nos. 7–10 are merely those in which the works begin.

and orchestra.[4] Published 1911 (Vienna, U.E.)

First perf.: Munich, 12 Sept. 1910; soloists: Gertrud Förstel, Marta Winternitz-Dorda, Irma Koboth, Otillie Meyzger, Tilly Koenen, Felix Senius, Nicola Geisse-Winkel, Richard Mayr; Leipzig Riedelverein, Vienna Singverein, Munich Central School Children's Chorus, Festival Orchestra (Mahler); first perf. in Britain: Queen's Hall, London, 15 April 1930, B.B.C. Symphony Orchestra, B.B.C. National Chorus, boys of Southwark Cathedral and others (Wood), with Elsie Suddaby, May Blyth, Irene Mordern, Muriel Brunskill, Clara Serena, Walter Widdop, Harold Williams and Robert Easton; first U.S. perf.: Philadelphia, 2 March 1916 (Leopold Stokowski).

1909–10 Symphony No. 9 in D major. Published 1912 (Vienna U.E.).

First perf.: Vienna, 26 June 1912, Vienna Philharmonic (Bruno Walter); first perf. in Britain (also broadcast): Manchester, 27 Feb. 1930, The Hallé Orchestra (Sir Hamilton Harty); first London performance: Queen's Hall, 7 Feb. 1934, B.B.C.S.O. (Boult); first U.S. performance: Boston, 16 Oct. 1931, Boston S.O. (Koussevitzky).

1910 Symphony No. 10 in F sharp major. Left unfinished. Sketches published in facsimile 1924 (Berlin, Paul Szolnay Verlag). Movements 1 and 3 published 1951 (New York, Assoc. Music Publishers).

First perf. of *Adagio* and *Purgatorio*: Vienna, 14 Oct. 1924, Vienna Philharmonic (Franz Schalk); first perf. in Britain: *Adagio*, B.B.C. broadcast, 20 Nov. 1948, B.B.C.S.O. (Hermann Scherchen); *Adagio* and *Purgatorio*, Royal Festival Hall, London, 30 Nov. 1955, Royal Philharmonic Orchestra (Richard Austin); first U.S. perf.: Erie, 6 Dec. 1949, Erie S.O. (Fritz Mahler).

Deryck Cooke performing version: first perf. (both *Scherzos* incomplete), B.B.C. broadcast, 19 Dec. 1960, Philharmonia Orchestra (Berthold Goldschmidt); (complete) Royal Albert Hall, London, 13 Aug. 1964, London Symphony Orchestra (Goldschmidt);

[4] The nickname 'Symphony of a Thousand' was true at Munich where over 1,000 performers were on the platform, comprising orchestra of over 150, the soloists, choruses of 500 voices and children's choir of 350.

(revised) Royal Festival Hall, London, 15 Oct. 1972, New Philharmonia (Wyn Morris); first U.S. perf.: Philadelphia, 5 Nov. 1965, Philadelphia Orchestra (Ormandy). Published 1976 (Assoc. Music Publishers, N.Y. and Faber Music, London).

JUVENILIA AND FRAGMENTARY WORKS
(All unpublished)

PROJECTED BUT UNCOMPLETED OPERAS

1875 *Herzog Ernst von Schwaben* (libretto by J. Steiner, probably based on Uhland)

1879–80(?) *Die Argonauten* (libretto by Mahler, probably based on Grillparzer)

1880–90 *Rübezahl* (libretto by Mahler)

ORCHESTRAL

1876–8 Symphony (rehearsed at Vienna Conservatory)

1876–8 Symphony in A minor (three movements in MS.)

CHAMBER MUSIC

1876 *Sonata for violin and pianoforte.* Performed Jihlava, 31 July 1876 (Mahler, pianist, Richard Schraml, violin).

1876 *Pianoforte Quintet in A minor* (first movement awarded prize at Vienna Conservatory, 1 July 1876). First perf.: Jihlava, 12 Sept. 1876 (Mahler, pianist).

1876 *Pianoforte Quartet in A minor* (one movement). First broadcast: Station WBAI, New York, 1962; first public performance: London, Purcell Room, 1 June 1968, Albert Landa (pianoforte) and Nemet Ensemble; first U.S. public performance: Cultural Center, New York, 17 Feb. 1973, Thomas Muraco (pianoforte) and violinist, violist and cellist of Concord Quartet.

1878 *Pianoforte Quintet (Scherzo).* Performed Vienna Conservatory, 11 July 1878 (Mahler, pianist).

INCIDENTAL MUSIC

For *Der Trompeter von Säkkingen* by Josef Viktor von Scheffel. For orchestra. First performance: Hoftheater, Cassel, 23 June 1884 (Mahler).

ARRANGEMENTS AND EDITIONS

J. S. Bach: Suite for Orchestra in four movements

    1. Overture in B minor (from Suite No. 2)
    2. Rondeau and Badinerie in B minor (from Suite No. 2)
    3. Air in D (from Suite No. 3 in D major)
    4. Gavotte in D (from Suite No. 3 in D major)

First perf.: New York, 25 Nov. 1909, N.Y.P.O. (Mahler, who also played *continuo* on pianoforte with action altered to resemble powerful harpsichord). Published 1911 (New York, Schirmer).

Bruckner: Symphony No. 3, pianoforte arrangement for four hands (Vienna, Rättig, 1878).

Mozart: *The Marriage of Figaro* (1906). Published 1908 (Leipzig, C. F. Peters). Recitatives for judgement scene.

Weber: Completion of *Die drei Pintos* (libretto in collaboration with K. von Weber). First perf.: Leipzig, 20 Jan. 1888, Mahler). First perf. in England: London, to April 1962, cond. by David Lloyd-Jones. Published 1888 (Leipzig, C. F. Kahnt Nachf.).
Euryanthe (new libretto by Mahler), 1903–4.
Oberon (new libretto by Mahler), 1906. Published 1919 (Vienna, U.E.)

Rescorings by Mahler of the Schumann symphonies and of several Beethoven works have not been published. Mahler's annotated scores of his own works and of works by Beethoven, Schubert, Schumann and others were presented to Southampton University by Miss Anna Mahler in March 1973.

It is important to remember that Mahler said: 'I have made these retouchings for myself, not for anyone else. When I conduct, I can take responsibility for them.'

Appendix C   Personalia

Adler, Guido (1855–1941), Austrian musicologist who founded and was first director of the influential Institute for Music History at Vienna University, where he succeeded Hanslick as professor of musicology (1898–1927). Pupil of Bruckner and author of a study of Mahler published in a year book in 1914 and as a book in 1916. Knew Mahler from his student days onwards.

Barbirolli, Sir John (1899–1970), English conductor who in the last twenty years of his life regularly conducted Mahler symphonies throughout the world. Recorded Nos. 1, 5, 6 and 9; and privately owned tapes exist of his outstanding interpretations of Nos. 2, 3 and 7.

Bauer-Lechner, Natalie (1858–1921), Austrian violinist who was a close friend of Mahler and his sisters up to the time of his marriage. Her *Memories of Mahler* (1923) is indispensable.

Berliner, Arnold (1862–1942), physicist who became a close friend of Mahler in Hamburg in 1891 and remained an intimate. He committed suicide in Berlin on hearing that the Nazis intended to deport him.

Bernstein, Leonard (b. 1918), American conductor (especially of New York Philharmonic) who has recorded all Mahler's symphonies and *Das Lied von der Erde* (with baritone instead of contralto).

Bodanzky, Artur (1877–1939), violinist in Vienna Opera orchestra who became an assistant conductor during Mahler régime. He was devoted to Mahler and his music. Settled in 1915 in United States where, until his death, he was chief German conductor at the Metropolitan Opera.

Busoni, Ferruccio (1866–1924). Composer, conductor, writer and virtuoso pianist who first met Mahler in Leipzig in 1887 and later was soloist with him in concerto performances in Hamburg, Vienna and New York. Mahler conducted several of Busoni's compositions.

Buths, Julius (1851–1920), German conductor of remarkably wide tastes whose pioneering work at the Lower Rhine Festival helped to win a hearing for Mahler, Strauss, Elgar and Delius.

Cardus, Sir Neville (1889–1975), English music critic and author whose championship of Mahler's cause never wavered. Published a volume of analysis of Mahler's first five symphonies, but his masterpiece is his essay on Mahler which first appeared in *Ten Composers* (1945).

Chantemesse, André (1851–1919), French physician and expert on bacteriological infections to whom Mahler went in Paris in April 1911. Associated with Pasteur Institute.

Chvostek, Franz (1864–1944), Viennese physician who treated Mahler in May 1911. Expert on blood diseases.

Conried, Heinrich (1848–1909), manager of the Metropolitan Opera, New York, 1903–8, who persuaded Mahler to work in the United States.

Cooke, Deryck (1919–76), English music critic, scholar and author specializing in Mahler, Wagner and Delius. His book *The Language of Music* is highly stimulating. Made an invaluable contribution to Mahlerian research through his performing version of the Tenth Symphony.

Damrosch, Walter (1862–1950), American conductor of German origin who, while conductor of New York Symphony Society 1885–1927, did remarkable work on behalf of contemporary composers. He first encountered Mahler at Hamburg in 1895 when he was impressed by a *Meistersinger* at the opera there.

Dehmel, Richard (1863–1920), poet whose work was set to music by several of Mahler's contemporaries including Richard Strauss and Reger. His poem *Verklärte Nacht* inspired Schoenberg's string sextet of that name.

Fremstad, Olive (1871–1951), American soprano of Swedish origin who was leading exponent of Wagnerian rôles at the Metropolitan, New York, until 1914.

Fried, Oskar (1871–1941), German conductor who knew Mahler and became an enthusiastic interpreter of his symphonies in the years between the wars. Mahler appears to have regarded him with tolerant condescension.

Gropius, Walter (1883–1969), distinguished and influential architect, director of the Bauhaus Academy (1918–28). He was the cause of Mahler's 1910 matrimonial crisis. Alma Mahler married him in 1915 but the union was short-lived. In 1934 he settled in England and went to the U.S. in 1937.

Groves, Sir Charles (b. 1915), the first English conductor to perform all Mahler's symphonies, including the Cooke version of the Tenth, with his orchestra, the Royal Liverpool Philharmonic. This he did in the 1960s.

Gutheil-Schoder, Marie (1874–1935), soprano who was one of the outstanding singer-actresses of Mahler's Vienna régime. She became a notable Elektra.

Haitink, Bernard (b. 1929), Dutch conductor of the Amsterdam Concertgebouw Orchestra since 1964 who has recorded Mahler's nine symphonies and the *Adagio* of the Tenth.

Hellmesberger, Joseph (1828–93), Austrian conductor and violinist (leader of a string quartet) who was director of the Vienna Conservatory from 1851 until his death. His son Joseph (1855–1907) was also a violinist and a conductor of ballet and was for a short time conductor of the Vienna Philharmonic after they had rid themselves of Mahler.

Jahn, Wilhelm (1834–1900), conductor of the Vienna Hofoper from 1881 to 1897, when he was succeeded by Mahler.

Klemperer Otto (1885–1973), German conductor who worked with Mahler and attended all rehearsals for the first performances of Symphonies Nos. 7 and 8. His interpretations of Mahler were notable for clarity and absence of excessive expression. His opinion of Mahler the conductor was unequivocal: 'Toscanini was the greatest conductor of his generation, but Mahler was a hundred times greater.'

Křenek, Ernst (b. 1900), Austrian composer who was at one time married to Mahler's daughter Anna and prepared the first performing version (1924) of *Adagio* and *Purgatorio* of Symphony No. 10.

Krzyżanowski, Rudolf (?1859–1911), fellow student of Mahler at Vienna Conservatory who became court conductor at Weimar, 1898–1907. Mahler's assistant at Hamburg, 1896–7.

Langford, Samuel (1863–1927), music critic of the *Manchester Guardian* from 1905 until his death. It can justifiably be claimed that he was the first English critic to appreciate Mahler at his real worth, as is shown by these extracts from his obituary of Mahler published on 19th May 1911 (p. 9): 'The greatest of present-day symphonists . . . While in a sense [his music] is thoroughly popular, it has so far missed popularity because it was not designed for it. . . . Mahler is as lightfooted as the most alert worldling could be. He is never in a hurry. Almost more than that of any other composer, his music may be said to dance. . . . In his Third Symphony Mahler first shows himself a composer who can break bounds with an air of transcendent genius.' Langford attended the great 1920 Mahler Festival in Amsterdam and his notices of it are still worth reading.

Lipiner, Siegfried (1856–1911), philosopher, poet and friend of Nietzsche. Known to Mahler from student days, but the friendship cooled under Alma's influence.

Marschalk, Max (1863–1940), German critic and composer, brother-in-law of the playwright Gerhart Hauptmann. Mahler wrote of him in 1896: 'He knows and understands my work better than anybody.'

Mengelberg, Willem (1871–1951), Dutch conductor of the Concertgebouw Orchestra of Amsterdam, 1895–1945, and at one time of the New York Philharmonic. A passionate advocate of Mahler, who said of him in 1906: 'There's no one else I could entrust a work of mine to with entire confidence.' Performed all Mahler's major works at the festival in Amsterdam, 1920. During the 1939–45 war he collaborated with the Nazis, who had banned Mahler's music and removed the Jews from the Concertgebouw.

Mildenburg, Anna von (1872–1947), Austrian soprano noted for her Isolde, Brünnhilde and Fidelio. In Mahler's Hamburg and Vienna companies. Married the poet Hermann Bahr in 1909.

Mitchell, Donald (b. 1925), English publisher and critic, authority on Britten. His *Mahler: The Early Years* and *The Wunderhorn*

Years are detailed studies. He also edited the second English edition of Alma Mahler's *Gustav Mahler: Memories and Letters*.

Pfitzner, Hans (1869–1949), German composer and conductor of Romantic music whose opera *Die Rose vom Liebesgarten* Mahler conducted in Vienna.

Pollini, Bernhard (1838–97), German tenor who became a noted theatre-manager, combining adventurous policy with profit. Manager of Hamburg Opera from 1873.

Richter Hans (1843–1916), Hungarian-born conductor who became a noted Wagnerian and conducted the first *Ring* cycle, 1876. Conductor of Vienna Opera, 1880–98, and of Hallé Orchestra, Manchester, 1899–1911.

Roller, Alfred (1864–1935), stage-designer who worked with Mahler in Vienna from 1903 and created famous productions of Mozart, Beethoven, Wagner and Gluck.

Rosé, Arnold (1863–1946), leading violinist, Vienna Philharmonic and Opera Orchestras, for fifty-seven years. He founded and led the Rosé Quartet. He married Mahler's sister Justine in 1902. She died in 1938, the year Rosé fled to London, where he lived until his death. Their daughter Alma was a victim of the Gestapo; their son Alfred (b. 1902) became an American citizen. Arnold's brother Edward (1855–1942), a cellist, married in 1898 Mahler's youngest sister Emma, who died in 1933.

Rückert, Friedrich (1788–1866), German Romantic poet who had a keen interest in Turkish and Oriental verse-forms. Several composers set his work to music.

Schalk, Franz (1863–1931), Austrian conductor who became assistant to Mahler at the Vienna Hofoper in 1900 and was director, 1918–1929. Mahler regarded him as pedestrian and incompetent and suspected him of intrigue. Closely associated with Bruckner's symphonies.

Schoenberg, Arnold (1874–1951), Austrian composer whose 'system of composing with twelve notes' revolutionized music in 1923. Beginning as a violent opponent of Mahler's music, he rapidly became an ardent champion.

Seidl, Arthur (1863–1928), German music critic and teacher who was an influential propagandist for Mahler, Strauss and others.

Mahler

Solti, Sir Georg (b. 1912), Hungarian conductor, now naturalized Briton. Has recorded nine of Mahler's symphonies, including notably a magnificent performance of the Eighth.

Specht, Richard (1870–1932), Austrian music critic and essayist who wrote biographies of Mahler, Strauss, Brahms and Puccini. Published analyses of Mahler's late works. It was to Specht at Munich in 1910 that Mahler described his Eighth as 'a gift to the nation'.

Stein, Erwin (1886–1958), Austrian music-critic who settled in London. His book *Orpheus in New Guises* contains valuable essays on Mahler; and he has left vivid detailed descriptions of Mahler's Viennese opera productions.

Walter, Bruno (1876–1962), Austrian conductor who was assistant to Mahler in Hamburg and Vienna, a close friend and for the rest of his life a fervent advocate. His interpretations were perhaps softer-centred than is now fashionable, but they are an irreplaceable link with the composer.

Weingartner, Felix von (1863–1942), succeeded Mahler as director of the Vienna Hofoper in 1907 and became one of the world's leading conductors of his day.

Wood, Sir Henry J. (1869–1944), English conductor of extraordinarily catholic and adventurous taste who was the first to conduct a Mahler symphony (No. 1) in England and later conducted the first English performances of Symphonies 4, 7 and 8 and *Das Lied von der Erde*.

Zemlinsky, Alexander von (1871–1942), Austrian conductor and composer who taught Schoenberg and became his brother-in-law A close friend of Alma Mahler. His opera *Es war einmal* was conducted by Mahler in Vienna in 1900. He went to America in 1938.

Zichy, Count Géza (1849–1924), Hungarian composer and one-armed pianist who had been a Liszt pupil. Intendant of Budapest Opera, 1891–4.

Zuckerkandl, Emil (1849–1910), Viennese anatomist who was a close friend of Alma Mahler's stepfather, the painter Carl Moll. His wife Bertha was related by marriage to Paul and Georges Clemenceau, both of whom were drawn into the Mahler circle.

Appendix D   Select Bibliography

Adler, Guido, *Gustav Mahler* (Vienna-Leipzig, 1916).
Barford, Philip, *Mahler Symphonies and Songs* (B.B.C. Music Guides, London, 1970).
  'Mahler: A thematic archetype' (*Music Review*, Vol. 21, No. 4, November 1960).
Bauer-Lechner, Natalie, *Erinnerungen an Gustav Mahler* (Leipzig-Vienna-Zürich, 1923). English ed. trans. Dika Newlin, ed. and annotated by Peter Franklin, *Recollections of Gustav Mahler* (London, 1980).
Bekker, Paul, *Mahlers Sinfonien* (Berlin, 1921).
  Die Symphonie von Beethoven bis Mahler (Berlin, 1918).
Berg, Alban, *Letters to his Wife*, trans. and annotated by Bernard Grun (London 1971, German ed., 1965).
Blaukopf, Herta, (ed.) *Gustav Mahler Richard Strauss Briefwechsel 1888–1911* (Munich, 1980). Eng. trans. Edmund Jephcott, *Gustav Mahler Richard Strauss Correspondence 1888–1911* (London, 1984).
Busoni, Ferruccio, *Letters to his Wife*, trans. Rosamond Ley (London, 1938).
Cardus, Sir Neville, *Gustav Mahler: his Mind and his Music*, Vol. I: *The First Five Symphonies* (London, 1965).
  'Mahler' in *Ten Composers* (London, 1945), reprinted in *A Composers' Eleven* (London, 1958).
Carner, Mosco, *Of Men and Music: collected essays and articles* (London, 1944).
Cooke, Deryck, *Gustav Mahler* (B.B.C. publication, London 1960).
  Mahler's Eighth Symphony (Royal Liverpool Philharmonic Society, Liverpool, 1964).
  'Mahler's Unfinished Symphony' (*The Listener*, 15 Dec. 1960).
  'Mahler's Tenth Symphony: sonority, texture and substance' (*Composer*, No. 16, July 1965).
  Gustav Mahler, an Introduction to his Music (London, 1980).

De la Grange, Henri Louis, 'Mistakes about Mahler' (*Music and Musicians*, Vol. 21, No. 2, October 1972).

Mahler, Vol. I (New York, 1973; London, 1974).

Del Mar, Norman, *Richard Strauss: a critical commentary on his life and works*, Vol. I (of three) (London, 1962).

Mahler's Sixth Symphony, a Study (London, 1980).

Engel, Gabriel, *Gustav Mahler: Song-Symphonist* (New York, 1932).

Gartenberg, Egon, *Mahler, the Man and his Music* (New York and London, 1978).

Heyworth, Peter (ed.), *Conversations with Klemperer* (London, 1973).

Holbrook, David, *Gustav Mahler and the Courage To Be* (London, 1975).

Jones, Ernest, *Sigmund Freud, Life and Work*, Vol. II (London, 1955).

Karpath, Ludwig, *Begegnung mit dem Genius* (Vienna-Leipzig, 1934).

Keller, Hans, 'The Unpopularity of Mahler's Popularity' (*The Listener*, 15 April 1971).

Keener, Andrew D., *Gustav Mahler as Conductor* (*Music and Letters*, Vol. 56, Nos. 3–4, 1975).

Klemperer, Otto, *Meine Erinnerungen an Gustav Mahler* (Zürich, 1960). English ed., *Memories of Mahler* (London, 1964).

Kolodin, Irving, *The Story of the Metropolitan Opera, 1883–1950* (New York, 1953).

Kralik, Heinrich von, *Das grosse Orchester. Die Wiener Philharmoniker und ihre Dirigenten* (Vienna, 1952).

Langford, Samuel (ed. Cardus), *Music Criticisms* (London, 1929).

Mahler, Alma Maria, *Gustav Mahler: Erinnerungen und Briefe* (Amsterdam, 1940).

English ed., *Gustav Mahler: Memories and Letters* (trans. Basil Creighton) (London, 1946); 2nd (enlarged) ed., edited with introduction by Donald Mitchell (London, 1968).

(ed.), *Gustav Mahler Briefe, 1879–1911* (Berlin-Vienna-Leipzig, 1924). For English edition see under Martner, Knud.

Introduction to facsimile of Symphony No. 10 (Vienna, 1924).

Martner, Knud (ed.) *Selected Letters of Gustav Mahler*, trans. Eithne Wilkins, Ernst Kaiser and Bill Hopkins; orig. ed. selected by Alma Mahler, enlarged and with new intro., illus. and notes.

(London, 1979).

Matthews, Colin, *Mahler at Work: Aspects of the Compositional Process* (Univ. of Sussex, diss., 1978).

Mildenburg, Anna von, *Erinnerungen* (Vienna, 1920).

Mitchell, Donald, *Gustav Mahler: the Early Years* (London, 1958, rev. 1980).

    The Wunderhorn Years (London, 1975).

    (ed.), English 2nd ed. of A. M. Mahler's *Gustav Mahler: Memories and Letters* (London, 1968); 3rd ed. enlarged with new appendix and chronology by D. Mitchell and Knut Martner (London, 1973).

    'About Mahler's Early Symphonies' (*The Listener*, 26 Feb. 1959).

    'Early and Mature Mahler' (*The Listener*, 25 October 1962)

Newlin, Dika, *Bruckner-Mahler-Schoenberg* (New York, 1947).

Prawy, Marcel, *The Vienna Opera* (London, 1969).

Redlich, Hans Ferdinand, *Bruckner and Mahler* (London, 1955, revised 1963).

    'Gustav Mahler' (entry in Vol. VIII, *Die Musik in Geschichte und Gegenwart*, Cassel-Basle-London-New York, 1960).

Reich, Willi, *Schoenberg: a critical biography*, trans. Leo Black (London, 1971).

Reilly, Edward R., *Gustav Mahler und Guido Adler: zur Geschichte einer Freundschaft* (Vienna, 1978), in Eng. as *Gustav Mahler and Guido Adler: Records of a Friendship* (Cambridge, 1982).

Roller, Alfred, *Die Bildnisse von Gustav Mahler* (Vienna-Leipzig, 1922).

Specht, Richard, *Gustav Mahler* (Berlin-Leipzig, 1913).

    Gustav Mahler (Berlin, 1905).

Stefan, Paul, *Gustav Mahler: eine Studie über Persönlichkeit und Werk* (Munich, 1910, revised 1912 and 1920). English ed. trans. Edward Clark (New York, 1913).

Stein, Erwin, *Orpheus in New Guises* (London, 1953).

    'Mahler and the Vienna Opera' in *The Opera Bedside Book*, ed. H. Rosenthal (London, 1965).

Truscott, Harold, 'Gustav Mahler' in *The Symphony*, Vol. 2 (ed. R. Simpson) (London, 1967).

    'Some Aspects of Mahler's Tonality' (*Monthly Musical Record*,

Nov.–Dec. 1957).

Walker, Frank, *Hugo Wolf, a Biography* (London, 1951, revised 1968).

Walter, Bruno, *Gustav Mahler* (Vienna-Leipzig-Zürich, 1936). 1st English ed. trans. James Galston (London, 1937); 2nd English ed. trans. supervised by Lotte Walter Lindt (London, 1958). *Theme and Variations, an Autobiography*, trans. James Galston (London, 1947).

Wellesz, Egon, 'The Symphonies of Gustav Mahler' (*Music Review*, Vol. I, Nos. 1 and 2, 1940).

Whaples, Miriam K., *Mahler and Schubert's A minor Sonata, D.784* (*Music & Letters*, Vol. 65, No. 3, 1984).

Wiesmann, Sigrid, (ed.) *Gustav Mahler und Wien* (Stuttgart and Zürich, 1976) Eng. ed. *Gustav Mahler in Vienna* (London, 1977).

Appendix E   Mahler's 're-touchings' of Beethoven

In February 1900 Mahler caused a printed explanation of his 're-touchings' of Beethoven's symphonies—and specifically the Ninth—to be distributed among the Vienna Philharmonic audience after he had been severely criticized for attempting to 'improve' Beethoven. In it he said:

> ... Because of his total deafness, Beethoven had lost the essential intimate contact with the reality of physical sound in the world just at the time in his creative development when a very powerful increase in understanding urged him to find new ways of expression and towards hitherto unthought-of drastic treatment of orchestration.

190

Just as well known as this fact is the other, namely, that the nature of the brass instruments of his time excluded the proper formation of succeeding notes which are needed for the formation of a melody. Just this very lack of perfection led to the improvement in the manufacture of these instruments and it would be a crime not to use them to give a more perfect rendering of Beethoven's works. Richard Wagner, who all his life by word and deed was passionately trying to rescue Beethoven's works from abysmal performances which had become almost unbearable, in his article 'On the Correct Performance of Beethoven's Ninth' indicates how to conduct this work in the way Beethoven had intended it to be heard, and most conductors have followed Wagner's advice.

The conductor of today's concert [i.e. Mahler] . . . does not differ in essentials from the limits drawn by Wagner. Nobody could possibly call this a re-orchestration or, still worse, an 'improvement' of Beethoven's composition. The customary increase in the number of stringed instruments has made it equally necessary to increase the number of wind instruments, and this was done solely to balance the volume of sound and not to give instruments a new significance. This point, as with any other concerning the interpretation of this work, in parts as well as in whole, can be proved to be correct by study of the score. This will lead to the conviction that the conductor . . . did not allow either 'tradition' or instinct to creep into it: he was determined not to sacrifice one iota of what the Master demands and did not allow any particle to become lost in the welter of sound.

Index

Index

Index

Schwarz, Gustav, 7n
Scotti, Antonio, 58, 59
Seidl, Anton, 62n
Seidl, Arthur, 29, 40, 97, 185
Sembrich, Marcella, 58, 59
Shaw, Bernard, 78, 110, 160
Shawe-Taylor, Desmond, 79–80
Shostakovich, Dmitri, 1, 159
Sibelius, Jean, 1, 55, 63, 159
Sistermans, Anton, 173
Slansky, Ludwig, 17
Slezak, Leo, 33, 59
Smetana, Bedřich, 21, 59
Solti, Sir Georg, 133, 186
Specht, Richard, 152, 186
Spiering, Theodore, 61, 63, 66
Stägemann, Max, 17
Stein, Erwin, 35–6, 37, 109 and n, 125, 186
Steiner, Joseph, 11, 12, 120, 179
Stockhausen, Karlheinz, 1
Stransky, Josef, 62n
Strauss, Johann, 147
Strauss, Richard, 1, 35, 40–1, 47, 51 and n, 62–3, 65, 75, 85, 97, 122
Stravinsky, Igor, vi, 2, 55, 157, 158

Tchaikovsky, Peter Ilyich, 21, 37, 59, 63, 92, 148, 149, 159
Thorborg, Kerstin, 139
Toblach, 69, 72, 147, 151
Toscanini, Arturo, 58, 59, 64, 65, 66
Treiber, Wilhelm, 15

Vaughan Williams, Ralph, vi, 22, 77–8, 84, 90, 101, 104, 130
Vienna Conservatory, 7, 8–13, 147, 179
Vienna Opera, 28, 29–30, 32–8, 47, 52–6

Vienna Philharmonic Orchestra, 9, 38–9, 40, 45, 50, 63, 94, 146, 174, 175, 178

Wagner, Richard, 9, 10, 11, 22, 33, 36, 37, 41, 77, 79, 84, 88, 97, 101, 144; Operas of: *Götterdämmerung*, 22; *Lohengrin*, 10, 29; *Die Meistersinger von Nürnberg*, 17; *Das Rheingold*, 17, 18, 22, *Rienzi*,' 17; *Der Ring des Nibelungen*, 9, 18, 22; *Siegfried*, 21, 22; 56, 58; *Tannhäuser*, 10; *Tristan und Isolde*, 22, 23, 35–6, 57–8, 59; *Die Walküre*, 17, 18, 22, 36, 58, 144
Walter, Bruno, v, 1, 24–6, 27, 30, 35, 37–8, 52, 53, 56, 67–8, 69, 70, 73, 75, 137, 151, 153, 159, 175, 178, 186
Weber, Hauptmann Carl von, 17, 180
Weber, Mathilde von, 17, 18
Webern, Anton von, 1, 120, 147
Weidemann, Friedrich, 33, 174
Weingartner, Felix von, 30, 53, 186
Werfel, Franz, 43
Wolf, Hugo, 8–9, 10, 13, 15, 29–30, 41
Wood, Sir Henry, 22, 173, 176, 177, 178, 186
Wüllner, Ludwig, 62, 140, 174
Wunderlich, Fritz, 138

Zemlinsky, Alexander von, 42, 45, 56, 152, 186
Zichy, Count, 19, 34, 186
Zuckerkandl, Emil and Bertha, 41, 186

196